OTHER WORLDS, OTHER BEINGS

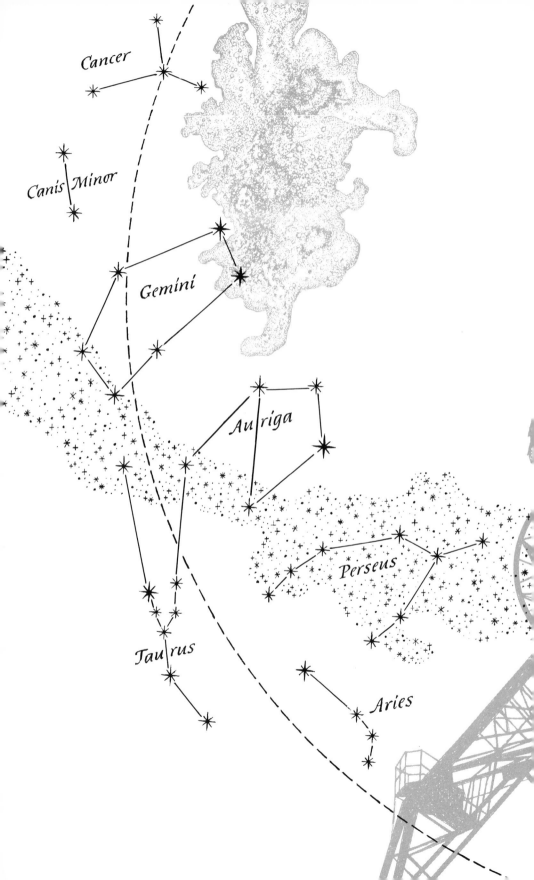

Cancer

Canis Minor

Gemini

Auriga

Perseus

Taurus

Aries

# OTHER WORLDS,
# OTHER BEINGS

By STANLEY W. ANGRIST

*DRAWINGS*

*BY ENRICO ARNO*

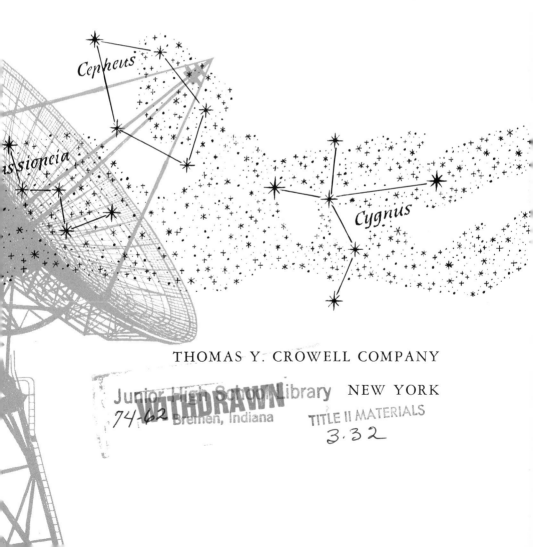

THOMAS Y. CROWELL COMPANY

NEW YORK

BY THE AUTHOR

*How Our World Came to Be*
*Other Worlds, Other Beings*

Photographs on pages 56, and 73 from the Hale Observatories.
Photographs on pages 60, 62, 68, 71, 96, 104, 106, and 113 courtesy of the
National Aeronautics and Space Administration.
Photograph on page 92 courtesy of Cornell University and the Bethlehem
Steel Corporation. The Arecibo Observatory is a national research center
operated by Cornell University under contract with the National Science
Foundation with partial support from the Advanced Research Projects Agency.

*Library of Congress Cataloging in Publication Data*
Angrist, Stanley W.
    Other worlds, other beings.
    SUMMARY: Examines the characteristics and needs of life on earth, the
possibilities and probabilities of life in outer space, and means of
communicating with extraterrestrial beings.
    Bibliography: p. 114
    1. Life on other planets.—Juvenile literature. [1. Life on other
planets]    I. Arno, Enrico, illus. II. Title.
QB54.A53      1973      577'.099      70-171001
ISBN 0-690-60205-7
1   2   3   4   5   6   7   8   9   10

TO SHIRLEY

# CONTENTS

# Chapter 1

# THE EXCITING STORY
# OF A FAINT RED DWARF

IN 1916 AN AMERICAN astronomer, Edward Emerson Barnard, discovered a very small and faint red star that recently began to change the way people think about their role in the universe. How could a star that is by any measure rather ordinary and millions of miles away bring about such an important change? The answer to that question has many parts, some of which will be explored in this book.

In 1968, fifty-two years after Barnard's faint red star was discovered, Peter van de Kamp, an astronomer at Swarthmore College, completed a long study of it. The results of that study, once they were understood, produced a lot of excitement among scientists. Van de Kamp used a special technique to observe Barnard's star over a period of twenty-five years. He concluded at the end of that time that Barnard's star has in orbit about it an invisible companion. This invisible companion—which completes its orbit about its sun, Barnard's star, in twenty-four years—was initially believed by many astronomers to be a planet. Even more exciting was the discovery that Barnard's star is the second closest star to our solar system— only six light-years away. That means it would take only six years for a radio message to get from earth to Barnard's star. For a star that is very close indeed.

Many astronomers today no longer believe the companion to Barnard's star to be a planet, but only a small, unseen star. In either case, planet or star, the discovery was still an important milestone, since it caused scientists the world over to begin thinking seriously about the possibility of life elsewhere in the universe.

It is true that Barnard's star is very old and relatively cool, and thus its planet, if its companion is a planet, is probably not habitable. But this unseen traveler, dragged through space by a faint red star, was the first body discovered outside of our solar system that was thought to be a planet.

How many of the stars that we can see in our heavens each night might also be surrounded by planets? And of these, do any have planets with some sort of life on them? Do any have planets with intelligent life on them?

These questions are not easy to answer. But there is now enough information available for man to begin to make intelligent, if tentative, guesses about the existence of other beings on other worlds. Because man has begun to take his first uncertain steps in space, it is now time for him to consider whether he is alone in the universe.

All the stars that can be seen with the naked eye, plus millions of other nearby stars too faint to be observed without telescopes, are in our galaxy. That faint whitish band of light that can be seen stretching across the heavens on a dark, clear night and that for thousands of years has been called "the Milky Way," is the visible part of our galaxy. The word *galaxy* is used to define a very large collection of stars and other heavenly bodies, more or less isolated in space. The galaxy to which we belong contains more than 100 billion other stars. Ten billion other galaxies, each containing about the same number of stars, are within range of our largest telescopes.

Stars are among the most important kinds of heavenly bodies. Almost all stars are gigantic nuclear furnaces that turn the lightest of all gases, hydrogen, into another very light gas, helium. The conversion of hydrogen to helium takes place by way of the fusion process that is used in the hydrogen bomb. The changing of hydrogen into helium in the sun, the star nearest to the earth, releases the tremendous amount of light and heat that make life on earth possible.

The one star in our galaxy that we know the most about is the sun. And to us it is a very special star. But when compared with the billions of stars in the galaxy, the following things must be noted about it: it is not an especially big star, nor is it one of the smaller stars; it is not the brightest star, nor one of the dimmer ones. In fact, in just about every respect it is average—in color, brightness, composition, and age. There are billions more like it scattered across our galaxy and in the other galaxies we can see. There is only one thing—but a very important thing indeed—that makes the sun special. It has nine planets, at least one of which is known to be inhabited by living, thinking beings.

If an ordinary star like our sun has nine planets in orbit

about it, and at least one of those planets carries intelligent life, how many other stars in the universe are accompanied by planets carrying intelligent life? How many other planets are there that carry some simpler form of life such as plants? The scientific way to try to answer such questions is through the branch of mathematics known as probability.

## Probability

When scientists try to estimate the likelihood of an event turning out a certain way, they state the *probability* for the outcomes of that event. If you toss a coin in the air, it will land with either "heads" or "tails" facing up. Those are the only two possible outcomes that can result from the tossing of a coin. How likely is it to land heads up? Your intuition tells you that half the time the coin will land heads up and half the time it will land tails up. The probability of observing a heads-up toss is then ½. With more complicated problems, however, you cannot use your intuition to determine the probability for various outcomes. You must resort to a more orderly procedure. The procedure followed to find the probability of an event is to divide the number of favorable outcomes (in the coin example there is only one favorable outcome for each player—heads up or tails up) by the total number of possible outcomes (in the coin example there are two—heads up and tails up). The probability, then, of a toss resulting in heads up is ½, as is the probability of its ending tails up. In this example the probability of observing a heads-up toss or a tails-up toss is the same.

A probability of one means that an event will certainly occur. A probability of zero means that an event will certainly *not* occur. In the coin-tossing example the probabilities for heads occurring and for tails occurring add up to one ($\frac{1}{2}$ + $\frac{1}{2}$ = 1), since it is certain that either heads or tails will occur.

If two events are independent—which means that the way one event turns out does not influence the way the other one turns out—the probability that both events will happen is found by multiplying their separate probabilities. For example, what is the probability of tossing a coin twice and having heads (or tails) come up twice in succession? Since each toss of the coin is independent of all other tosses of the coin, the multiplication rule holds. The probability of heads coming up on any single toss is $\frac{1}{2}$, and therefore the probability of heads occurring twice in a row is simply $\frac{1}{2} \times \frac{1}{2} = \frac{1}{4}$, which means that the probability of heads coming up both times in two successive tosses is one in four. This process of using the probability of a single event to find the probability of an event that depends on a number of single events may be continued indefinitely. Thus, the probability of heads (or tails) occurring three times in a row is one in eight ($\frac{1}{2} \times \frac{1}{2} \times \frac{1}{2} = \frac{1}{8}$).

## Probability of Habitable Planets

It is this method of probabilities that scientists have tried to use to estimate the likelihood of the existence of planets on which man would be able to live—that is, habitable planets. It should be kept in mind, however, that since almost none of the information used in making the relevant probability estimates on other homes for life is certain, the results of these probability calculations are far from precise. Still they can give us some idea about the number of habitable planets in the galaxy. A *habitable planet,* according to Stephen Dole, a scientist of the Rand Corporation who has done some of the most thorough research on this subject, would be a planet on which large numbers of people could live without needing excessive protection from the environment that exists on that planet. In other words, a planet that is habitable can supply all the physical requirements of human beings and provide an environment in which people can live comfortably and enjoyably. Dole studied this problem from man's point of view in that he was looking for planets on which people from earth would be comfortable; however, there might be a number of planets that man would not find habitable but that could support other forms of life—probably some simple animal and plant life similar to the algae and lichens found on earth. Therefore, Dole's estimate of the number of habitable planets is smaller than the total number of planets capable of harboring some form of life.

The job of determining the probability of there being planets capable of supporting life in the galaxy can be broken into two parts: first, it is necessary to determine in a rough way how many of the more than 100 billion stars in the galaxy are capable of having planets that might possibly support any kind of life in orbit about them; and second, it must be determined how many of those planets would meet all the more specific conditions that are believed to be necessary to support life.

The answer to the first part is to be found in what astronomers know about stars. Most of them agree that if a star is less than three-quarters the size of our sun or more than one and a half times bigger than our sun, it would probably not have planets with conditions suitable for life of any sort. If the stars are much smaller than our sun, they do not give out sufficient light and heat to support life. There are also other limitations that probably prohibit stars much smaller than our sun from having habitable planets; these will be discussed in Chapter 5. All stars are believed to go through an aging process in some ways similar to the aging process of humans. Stars that are much larger than our sun have lives less than about 3 billion years, which is probably not enough time to let habitable conditions develop on any planet in orbit about them. Dole estimated that "only" about 17 billion of the 100 billion or so stars in our galaxy are neither too large (and thus die too young) nor too small (and thus fail to give out enough heat and light) to have planets that are possibly habitable.

Making estimates of the number of habitable planets in the galaxy, of course, cannot be done with great mathematical accuracy at our present state of knowledge of the rest of the galaxy. Recall that there is no conclusive proof of the existence of even one planet outside the solar system.

Nevertheless, by using the idea of multiplying probabilities Dole was able to get the overall likelihood of finding planets suitable for man. Some scientists feel Dole's results are quite reasonable. After listing all the conditions he felt must be satisfied if a planet were to be habitable, Dole carefully studied each of the conditions he had set down. He estimated how likely it was for planets in our galaxy to satisfy each condition.

That is, he calculated (or in some cases guessed) a probability value for each of his listed conditions. Finally he multiplied together the estimated probabilities for each of the conditions and found an overall probability for the occurrence of habitable planets in our galaxy. The conditions that he listed, and then estimated probabilities for, were:

1.  A star of the "right" size must have planets in orbit about it. Obviously, this condition is the most important one concerning the occurrence of habitable planets in our galaxy. At the present time our understanding of the process of planet formation is not complete enough to say with any certainty how many stars in the galaxy have at least one planet in orbit about them. However, the fact that planets can and do form about stars is known with 100 percent certainty. Dole's estimate of at least one planet per star is considered by many astronomers to be too high. In the calculations made here it is assumed that only one star in each thousand has one or more planets in orbit about it.

2.  The angle at which the planet's equator is inclined to the plane of its orbit must be correct for its distance from its sun.

The earth's axis of rotation is inclined 23.5 degrees toward the imaginary plane in which it rotates about the sun. This produces long days and high temperatures in the summer in the Northern Hemisphere. It causes short days and low temperatures in the winter. But it has just the opposite effect in the Southern Hemisphere.

If a planet's pole of rotation is too greatly inclined toward its plane of rotation, it produces large regions of almost continual daylight in the summer and extended periods of almost continual darkness in the winter. This type of illumination pattern is very similar to what our polar regions experience.

This angle has a big effect on the sunlight received and the temperature extremes that will be attained on the planet's surface.

3. The planet must not be too far away from, or too close to, its sun. A planet's distance from its sun also strongly influences illumination and surface temperature.

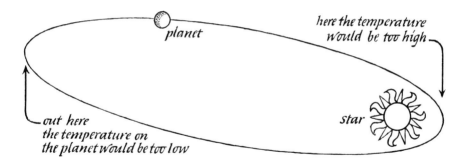

Greatly elongated planetary orbits produce temperature extremes on a planet.

4. The size of the planet must not be too great or too small. If too small, a planet will not have a strong enough gravitational pull to hold onto an atmosphere, which is necessary if the planet is to be habitable. If the planet is too large, the atmosphere would be so heavy and thick that it could not be breathed by humans.

5. The planet must not be following an orbit that is too stretched out. A greatly elongated orbit would cause large variations in the temperature on the surface, probably making the planet uninhabitable.

6. No second star must be close enough to make the planet uninhabitable. The gravitational pull of a second star can cause a planet to follow an orbit that would prohibit life; or the light and heat from a second star could produce temperatures too high for living organisms.

7. The planet must not turn too slowly. Planets that complete rotation in more than about ninety-six hours (4 earth days) might attain excessively high daytime temperatures and excessively low nighttime temperatures. However, certain types of atmosphere that might surround a planet could permit a very slowly rotating planet to be habitable.

8. The planet must be of the proper age. A planet less than 3 billion years of age would not have had sufficient time to develop complex life forms and the breathable atmosphere that human beings would need.

9. All other conditions being suitable, some form of life must have already developed on the planet. Dole reasoned that any planet man would find habitable would have some life already existing on it that would provide an oxygen-rich atmosphere. The life already present on the planet, perhaps some form of plant life, would be capable of releasing oxygen to the planet's atmosphere.

After assigning a probability to each of the nine conditions, Dole multiplied them together to get an overall probability of finding a habitable planet. If what many scientists believe is true—that is, that most stars do not have planets in orbit about them—then Dole's calculations must be modified as suggested earlier in point 1. Even after making that modification by assuming that only one in a thousand stars has one or more planets in orbit about it, the results of Dole's work are still, in some ways, startling. One out of every 26,000 of the 17 billion stars that are approximately the right size is estimated to have a habitable planet in orbit about it. This yields a little over 600,000 planets in our galaxy alone that are likely to have conditions under which man could live. Dole, it should be recalled, was seeking an estimate of how many planets are habitable. He did not try to estimate how many planets have some form of life on them but would still not be habitable by man. Thus this estimate of 600,000 habitable planets in our galaxy may be a very low one. Since there are billions of galaxies in the universe, each with its own quota of habitable planets and planets that cannot be called habitable but yet may carry some forms of life, the probability of the earth being the only home for life in the universe appears to be small.

However, it should be noted that just because a planet is termed habitable does not mean it will necessarily have intelligent life present on it. In fact, a number of scientists feel that this probability is quite low. Their reasoning is based on the observation that there are an enormous number of different paths along which organisms can evolve. George W. Beadle, the geneticist, indicates that the probability of an organism evolving with a nervous system like man's is extremely small. On earth, it has been only within the past 100,000 years or so, out of perhaps 2 to 3 billion years during which living things existed, that the presence of a highly intelligent species would have been apparent to a visitor from some other planet. It may be that, allowed enough time, such a species will eventually appear on a given habitable planet. However, its time of appearance is probably not highly predictable. If, through some unlucky accident, the human race became extinct, how long might it be before some other intelligent species would evolve from the existing animal species of the earth? There is no obvious answer to that question.

Can an estimate, then, be made of how many planets (if there are any) in our galaxy already carry intelligent life or life at all? Unfortunately the answer to this question must be no. But the calculations presented here indicate more than 600,000 habitable planets in our galaxy alone. Suppose for the sake of discussion that only one out of every thousand of these planets possesses life—that still gives us 600 homes for life to look for in our own little piece of the universe.

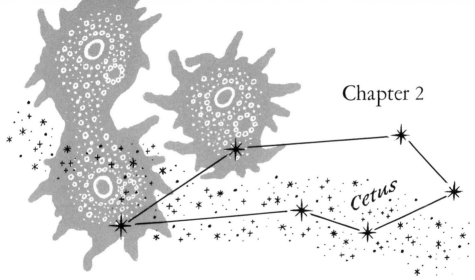

# Chapter 2

# WHAT LIFE IS MADE OF

IN ORDER to consider the probability of life existing elsewhere in the universe, it is first necessary to examine what is meant by the word *life* on earth, and whether we can use this definition of life for the rest of the universe. As Carl Sagan, an American astronomer, has pointed out, any child can tell the difference between a live puppy, a dead puppy, and a toy puppy. If that is the case, defining what is meant by life should be pretty simple. Unfortunately, for a number of reasons, it is not.

Scientists who have studied the characteristics of an object that is called living agree that it must possess, or once have possessed, the ability to grow, to reproduce, and to respond to changes in its environment. It also must exhibit continual chemical activity, commonly called *metabolism.* Furthermore, most biologists add to the list the ability to *mutate.* That is, a living thing must possess the ability to pass on a change in one or more of its characteristics to its offspring.

Taken separately, almost any of these properties can be found in the nonliving world. The flame of a candle exhibits continual chemical activity. Crystals of many salts or certain elements can show growth. An inflated balloon may be highly sensitive to a very slight stimulation from its surroundings. It is only when all of these characteristics are organized into a single entity or object that the object is said to be alive.

The different forms of life on earth are astounding—but all its forms are built around a small unit called the *cell*. Cells are the smallest units of living matter capable of extracting energy from food to use in carrying out cell activities such as respiration, growth, and reproduction. Many cells—for example, protozoans, various simple algae, and bacteria—are individuals able to live independently and to reproduce their own kind. Others live in colonies or in multicellular plants or animals in which there is a division of labor among the many cells. Cells, whether they are in bacteria or in an oak tree, are complicated arrangements of molecules. Molecules, in turn, are either simple or complex arrangements of atoms—the building blocks of the entire universe.

## Atoms and Molecules

All of the studies that scientists have made of the planets, the stars, and the thin gas drifting between the stars indicate that atoms and molecules are the same everywhere throughout the universe. Every bit of evidence that has been collected so far says that if an atom behaves in a certain way on earth it will behave the same way on Jupiter or in the neighborhood of Barnard's star. Hence a discussion of atoms and molecules is as important to the understanding of the chemistry of life elsewhere in the universe as it is to the understanding of the chemistry of life on earth. As man's exploration of space continues, he will look for certain kinds of molecules on the planets he and his instruments will visit. If he finds traces of certain molecular structures on these other worlds, he might be able to establish that living things are present or were present on them at some time during the past.

All ordinary matter is composed of atoms. They are tiny bits of matter far too small to be seen even with microscopes. Each atom consists of smaller particles called neutrons, protons, and electrons. Some atoms are relatively big and some are

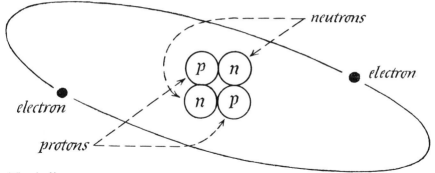

The helium atom

small. The size of an atom is mainly determined by the number of protons and neutrons that make up its nucleus and the number of electrons that form the electron cloud around the nucleus. The number of protons in the nucleus determines what kind of atom it is: for example, if it is an atom of hydrogen it has one proton in its nucleus; if it is an atom of silver it has forty-seven protons in its nucleus. Any substance com-

posed only of atoms having the same number of protons in the nucleus is called an *element*. Elements cannot be separated into simpler substances by ordinary chemical methods.

The *proton* is the positively charged particle found in the nucleus of an atom. The *neutron* is a second type of tiny particle found in the nucleus. It carries no electric charge. Surrounding the nucleus is the same number of *electrons* as there are protons in the nucleus. Electrons carry a negative charge. The charge on a particle tells how the particle would behave if, for example, it were possible to bring it near a negative terminal on a battery. A proton, carrying a positive charge, would be attracted to a negative terminal, since opposite charges attract each other. An electron, carrying a negative charge, would be pushed away from the negative terminal, since like charges repel each other. A neutron, carrying no charge, would neither be attracted nor repelled.

Early in this century it was believed that the atom resembled a tiny solar system, with the nucleus representing the sun and the electrons the orbiting planets. The modern picture of the atom is quite different from the original picture. Scientists now recognize that it is impossible to state precisely where the electron is with respect to the nucleus—it is only possible to predict where certain numbers of electrons will *probably* be found. For this reason electrons are now considered to form a "haze" around the nucleus.

Hydrogen, the simplest of all the atoms, has only one electron in orbit around its nucleus. Other kinds of atoms have progressively more electrons orbiting the nucleus. Chemists call the orbital paths located at different distances from the nucleus within a particular atom *shells*. It is well to keep in mind that in describing an atom in terms of orbits only a working model of the atom is being given. It does not, in any real sense, describe an atom as an atomic physicist might think about it.

Lithium has three protons in its nucleus and thus must have three electrons orbiting the nucleus. The shell closest to the nucleus of any atom can hold only two electrons, so the third electron must go into the second shell located further from the heart of the nucleus. In general, the first shell holds two electrons and the outermost shell never contains more than eight electrons; no shell between the first and last can ever hold more than thirty-two electrons.

Although atoms are electrically neutral in that they contain as many negative charges as positive charges, only a very few of them are not likely to interact (or react) with at least some other atoms.

The concept of shells is useful for explaining the behavior of atoms. When the outermost shell of an atom is filled with all the electrons it can hold, it is likely to be nonreactive toward other atoms. Atoms which have shells that do not contain all the electrons they can hold combine in such a way as to share electrons and thus produce an atomic combination that has a full complement of electrons in its shells.

For example, the hydrogen atom is highly reactive. That is, it will not remain alone if there is an opportunity for it to join other atoms. When two hydrogen atoms approach each other at a distance less than the diameter of a hydrogen atom, the two atoms interact by means of their orbiting electrons to form one complete shell. The shared shell now has two electrons in it and hence is considered full. By sharing each other's electrons, the two hydrogen atoms form a unit that is more stable and less likely to react chemically than a single hydrogen atom. This shared unit of two hydrogen atoms is called a

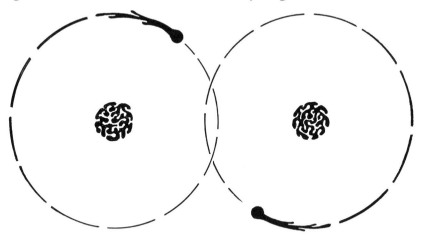

The interaction of two hydrogen atoms to form a hydrogen molecule

*hydrogen molecule.* A molecule of a substance is the smallest part of that substance that can exist separately. For example, a water molecule cannot exist with less than two atoms of hydrogen and one atom of oxygen.

When the outer shell of an atom is full, then that atom has no place to receive an electron and has none to donate. The gas neon, which is used in brightly lit signs seen in shopping districts, is composed of such complete atoms. A neon atom has its full complement of two electrons in its inner shell and eight electrons in its outer shell. Since a neon atom has no place to receive a shared electron, it cannot even join with another neon atom to form a neon molecule. A single atom of neon is also a molecule of neon. Substances that do not react easily are said to be *inert.*

Carbon is the basic element of life on earth. It has four electrons in its outer shell and combines readily with a number of other atoms. A special role is played by carbon in living organisms because it possesses, to a far greater extent than any other element, the power of combining with itself, as well as with other elements, to build up very large single molecules containing large numbers of atoms. It is these large, complex molecules containing carbon that form the basic structure of all living organisms on earth. It is for this reason that molecules built around carbon atoms are sometimes called *organic* molecules. Carbon atoms have the remarkable ability to combine with hydrogen and oxygen atoms in long chains of atoms that make up the four types of molecules found in all living plants and animals—the proteins, the nucleic acids, the fats, and the carbohydrates.

The molecules most frequently encountered in living things are proteins and nucleic acids. These are the largest and most complex of all known molecules. It has not been too surprising, then, to discover that molecules of proteins and of nucleic acids possess properties that are unknown in smaller and simpler molecules, including the ability to store large amounts of information. For example, stored within the nucleic acids found in a poodle is the information that would cause that poodle to give birth to another poodle and not a terrier, a goldfish, or an oak tree. Also stored in these special compounds is information that would determine the hair and eye color and thousands of other traits of the poodle's offspring. Cells, constructed of proteins, nucleic acids, and other complex molecules, are generally considered to be the first level of things that are without a doubt alive.

## Cells

Without cells there is no life. And just as life may take many forms, so may the nature and function of cells. Whatever its form, however it reacts, the cell is the basic unit of all living matter. Nature has placed in the tiny package we call a cell all the equipment necessary for the survival of life in a continually changing world. Most biologists believe that when

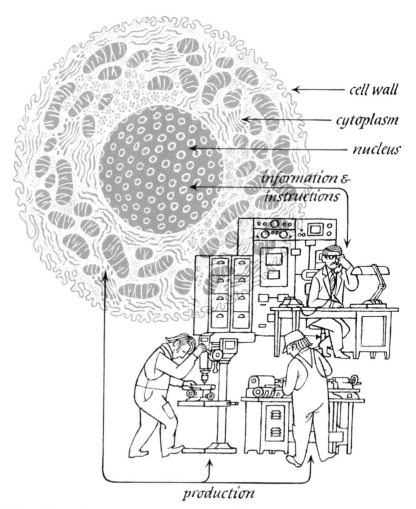

*cell wall*

*cytoplasm*

*nucleus*

*information & instructions*

*production*

The cell may be considered analogous to a factory. The nucleus contains the instructions and plans for carrying on the production in the cytoplasm.

and if life is discovered elsewhere, it too will be based on cells or cell-like structures not too different, at least in function, from the cells known on earth.

The structure of a cell is commonly divided into two parts —a *nucleus* and a surrounding layer of *cytoplasm.* The nucleus contains all the information describing the characteristics of the cell, and the cytoplasm is the region where most of the cell's living activities take place. Detailed studies of living cells indicate that the organizing centers of their growth and development are the *chromosomes,* the tiny threadlike bodies that are found within the cellular nucleus. Some biologists have compared the nucleus to the chief engineer's office in an individual factory, and the chromosomes to the file cabinets and bookshelves in which all the production plans and blueprints are stored.

Information storage in chromosomes is done by genes that determine all hereditary traits. Each chromosome bears hundreds of genes arranged in a line along its length. The key chemical compound of the gene is the nucleic acid known as *deoxyribonucleic acid,* or DNA for short. DNA contains a chemical compound called a *phosphate,* a sugar compound called *deoxyribose,* and four other compounds called *bases.* All sugar compounds are composed of atoms of carbon, hydrogen, and oxygen. Bases also use carbon atoms as their fundamental building blocks, to which are attached atoms of hydrogen, oxygen, and nitrogen. In DNA these molecules are arranged in units of phosphate-sugar-base–phosphate-sugar-base repeated thousands of times to form long, coiled chains. This fundamental arrangement is common to all DNA. The exact proportion of each of the four bases and the precise order in which they are arranged are unique for each kind of living thing. Each DNA molecule contains about 20,000 such phosphate-sugar-base units. A chromosome contains many thousands of DNA molecules. It is by the arrangement of the four bases along the DNA molecule that information is stored in much the same way that letters may be arranged to form words, and words arranged to form sentences, to store information on a page. Because there are so many different arrangements possible, countless numbers of genes can be formed. It is differences in genes that cause each of us to be slightly different even from our sisters or brothers.

One of the most remarkable features of this so-called genetic code is that it is the same for all plants and animals that have been studied so far, including viruses, bacteria, yeasts, several plant species, and various animals including man. Yet in spite of its great importance for the functioning of living organisms, DNA is present in extremely minute amounts; the total amount of DNA present in an adult man within his cell nuclei is about one teaspoonful.

In the surrounding layer of cytoplasm the cell engages in the manufacture of protein molecules made up of various combinations of carbon, hydrogen, nitrogen, oxygen, and usually sulfur. Proteins exist in all living things—in bacteria, in the leaves of plants, in bark and roots and in the cells that make up tissues and organs, in the muscle fibers, in skin and bone. The energy needed for the manufacturing processes of cell growth and for reproduction is extracted in the cytoplasm from food taken in by the cell.

Some cells are completely self-sufficient and are capable of living independently; single-celled creatures such as the amoeba and the paramecium are examples of these free-living units. Cells can also be specialists with only a single job to do; among these cells are included most of those that form the higher organisms. Their existence depends upon fitting into a rather complex community life with other cells. Such cells group together to form tiny creatures too small for you to see living on the leaf of the oak tree in your backyard, shrimp that cling to ancient rocks beneath the cold waters of the ocean, house spiders, robins, kangaroos, and men—in short the whole living world around us.

## Animal and Plant Cells

The evolution of plants and animals has come about only because cells were able to take on an enormous number of forms and duties. Cells found in green plants do many different things. Some form leaves that absorb energy from sunlight; others form roots; still others becomes pipes in the stem and bring food elements to various parts of the plant. The success of the plant growth process depends largely upon the cell walls of cellulose, which stiffen the whole organism so that leaves may rise into the sunlight and roots may dig deep into the soil.

Animal cells that hunt food developed the ability to move, and with it methods to defend themselves and to attack other cells. In organisms such as the hydra, a small jellyfish-like animal found in fresh water, the cells for offense, defense, and movement became grouped on the outside, while those for eating captured prey were grouped inside. From this simple beginning came the complex structures of the modern mammal, in which each of the four or five thousand different kinds of cells does its part in maintaining life in the whole animal.

More remarkable than their differences is the similarity between animal and plant cells. Both plant and animal cells are similar in the way they liberate energy, store information in their chromosomes, divide in reproduction processes, and undergo fertilization. Studies have shown that the makeup of the tail of the male reproductive cell (sperm) of a mammal or a fern is the same. In both plants and animals energy is packaged in special molecules called ATP (adenosine triphosphate).

Perhaps the most noteworthy feature of animal and plant cells on earth is the balance that has been struck between organisms made up of animal cells and organisms made up of plant cells. Their dependence on each other has proved to be beneficial to both. Most scientists believe that a similar balance between animal and plant cells will have been struck on other planets where life has flourished. It is, no doubt, this harmony in nature that has allowed 20,000 kinds of fishes to inhabit the seas and 1 million different species of animals to exist on the continents.


## Nature's Balance


Many of the animals on earth inhale air in order to extract oxygen from it, and then they exhale the gas carbon dioxide as a waste product. Carbon dioxide is a gas made up of an atom of carbon (C) and a molecule of oxygen ($O_2$); it is commonly written $CO_2$. Green plants when exposed to sunlight absorb carbon dioxide from the air and release oxygen into the air as a waste product. Animals use the oxygen they take in by reacting it with certain molecules taken from food to supply them with energy, while forming waste products like carbon dioxide, which are exhaled. This process is called *respiration*. Green plants in sunlight use the carbon dioxide waste products of animals, and water taken in by the plant's root system. The water is split into its components of hydrogen and oxygen;

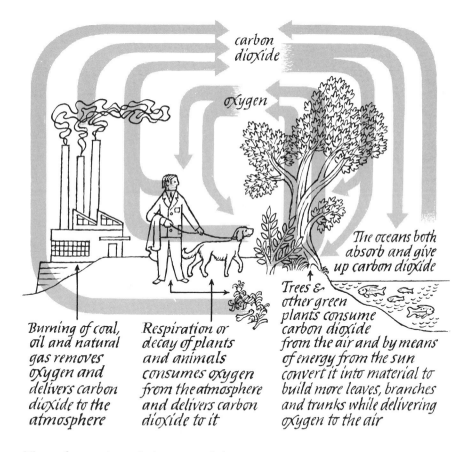

carbon dioxide

oxygen

The oceans both absorb and give up carbon dioxide

Burning of coal, oil and natural gas removes oxygen and delivers carbon dioxide to the atmosphere

Respiration or decay of plants and animals consumes oxygen from the atmosphere and delivers carbon dioxide to it

Trees & other green plants consume carbon dioxide from the air and by means of energy from the sun convert it into material to build more leaves, branches and trunks while delivering oxygen to the air

The carbon cycle, or balance struck between animals and plants during this process of *photosynthesis* the hydrogen is combined with the carbon dioxide to form organic molecules used in the plant's new growth, while the oxygen is released back into the air. In darkness, however, green plants may also release carbon dioxide into the air, as do non-green plants and many industrial processes that involve the burning of fossil fuels like coal, oil, and natural gas. All living organisms on earth participate in this exchange of oxygen and carbon dioxide, which is called the *carbon cycle.*

It should be pointed out, however, that certain foods can have energy removed from them—or metabolized—without using oxygen. Sugar, for example, can be reacted in such a way that it yields alcohol and carbon dioxide without consuming oxygen. In fact, this is what happens in the fermentation of grape juice into wine. This change is brought about by yeasts or other forms of cell life that supply enzymes, or transformers, whose presence makes possible a chemical change that would not otherwise take place. The process of fermentation is not a very efficient method of obtaining energy from food; it is far inferior to the respiration process used by all animals on earth. Therefore, it is not well suited to providing the energy required for the maintenance of life processes. However, fermentation is sometimes used in the cells found in the muscles of animals. For example, during periods of extreme exertion it is the fermentation process that produces certain energy-bearing molecules in the muscle. The capacity of this supplementary system to produce energy without oxygen is, of course, limited, and within a short period of time the body of the animal must settle the "oxygen debt" his muscle cells have created. That is why after a strenuous event you will see an athlete breathing deeply as his body tries to settle the "debt" created by his muscles. Fermentation is also the method employed by certain parasitic organisms that live in intestines where a plentiful supply of sugar is available. Such organisms do not need to provide energy to maintain their own temperatures, because they live a sheltered existence in an environment of uniform temperature supplied by their host. They are able to live without an oxygen supply, though they depend on a host who could not live without an oxygen supply. In an indirect way, then, they do depend on a supply of oxygen.

Much of the animal life found on the earth today is dependent upon a supply of oxygen to live. That the balance that has been struck between these animals and green plants in utilizing each other's waste products has been good cannot be denied; the millions of different species of plants and animals are the best evidence of this beneficial balance. However, most scientists believe that life did not originate in an oxygen-rich atmosphere like that found on earth today. The reason for this belief is that oxygen is a very reactive chemical; therefore, in an oxygen-rich atmosphere organic molecules over geological time would combine with the oxygen present in the atmosphere to produce carbon dioxide, nitrogen and water. The reactive tendency of oxygen would have prevented the evolution of the complex molecules out of which life ultimately evolved. It is for this reason that scientists believe that the atmosphere that surrounded the earth when life began was poor in oxygen.

# Chapter 3

Cygnus

# LIFE HERE AND LIFE THERE

ALL BIOLOGICAL LIFE on earth has been found to have the following major characteristics or properties:

1. It is made up of collections of different molecules that are mostly rather complex compounds of carbon; these collections contain a tremendous amount of stored information in large molecules such as deoxyribonucleic acid (DNA).

2. It reproduces itself accurately but has a small probability of producing a change in one or more of its characteristics, thereby causing long-term changes in a species.

3. It senses changes in the surroundings and reacts to them.

4. It maintains a shell or boundary that clearly separates the organism from its surroundings.

5. It utilizes one or more control systems to regulate its activities.

6. It utilizes energy from sources external to itself such as food or sunlight—that is, it experiences metabolism.

Is it reasonable to believe that life elsewhere in the universe must also possess each of the above characteristics? Most scientists believe that life on other worlds would not necessarily have every one. The following brief examination of these characteristics gives some additional information about the characteristics of life on earth, and what man now expects of life elsewhere.

## 1. Life Based on Carbon Atoms

A number of scientists have suggested that a biology might be discovered elsewhere that would be based on the element silicon instead of carbon. Silicon, with fourteen protons in its nucleus and fourteen electrons in orbit about the nucleus, also has the ability to build up complex molecules. In union with oxygen, silicon is the main component of the rocks that form the crust of the earth. Elemental silicon is not found in nature because it eagerly shares its outermost electrons with oxygen to form silicon dioxide. Silicon dioxide is commonly found in nature in the form of quartz crystals. Silicon and oxygen can join with magnesium and water to form long-chain substances like asbestos, which is used as a fireproofing material. Though the silicon atom can be the backbone for a number of long-chain molecular structures, it is still far less versatile than the carbon atom in its ability to make big, complicated molecules. N. V. Sidgwick, a noted English chemist, summed up the arguments against a silicon-based biology rather completely when he wrote:

Carbon is unique among the elements in the number and variety of the compounds which it can form. Over a quarter of a million compounds have already been isolated and described, but this gives a very imperfect idea of its powers, since it is the basis for all forms of living matter. Moreover, it is the only element which could occupy such a position. We know enough now to be sure that the idea of a world in which silicon could take the place of carbon as the basis for life is impossible; the silicon compounds have not the stability of those of carbon, and in particular it is not possible to form stable compounds with long chains of silicon atoms. [N. V. Sidgwick, *The Chemical Elements and Their Compounds*, Vol. I. New York: Oxford University Press, 1950.]

Sidgwick's argument summarizes fairly strongly the case for a carbon-based biology. Because it was written in 1950, however, it does not include what may be the most important point against a silicon-based biology: long-chain silicon molecules do not form nonrepeating bonds with other molecules which could be used as an information storage mechanism. The carbon-based DNA molecule does. Man has only recently begun to understand how information is stored in the DNA molecule built around the carbon atom. The concept of information storage by means of the arrangement and order of the atoms in the DNA molecule is extremely complicated and subtle. Without completely understanding how information is transmitted from one generation to the next in living things on earth, it is difficult for man to imagine, in any kind of detail, another system of information storage and transmittal that may be used in living objects on other worlds; however, it would be equally foolish, at this stage of man's understanding, to deny the possibility of other methods of information storage.

## 2 and 3. Reproduction, Mutation, and Evolution

Anything that is considered to be living must possess the ability to reproduce itself; if it did not have such an ability it would, of course, quickly become extinct. But almost as important as the ability to reproduce is the ability of an organism to slightly change from one generation to the next as it reproduces. This ability, called *mutation,* is what allows an organism to *evolve* from a single cell like the paramecium through a large number of small changes to a walking, talking, and thinking being capable of wondering about life on other worlds. Without the ability to mutate it is hard to imagine how the higher forms of life could ever have come into existence. The view most widely held today is that it is the powerful combination of mutation and evolution that has produced on earth the more complex forms of life known today.

A mutation is usually defined as an abrupt and heritable change in an organism's genetic material. Genetic material is considered to be either chromosomes or genes. Chromosomes are made up of DNA and special groups of proteins known as *histones.* Genes are simply part of a DNA molecule. Most mutations are harmful, but chance can cause an improvement in an organism's genetic material and thus improve its chances for survival.

A simple example of mutation and evolution might clarify this important idea concerning the development of any living group of organisms. Imagine a population of a particular kind of mouse called a deer mouse living in a wood lot. Each mouse carries stored within its chromosomes information that it will pass on to its offspring. One of these pieces of information controls the color of the mouse's coat, and any mouse with this particular information has a dark-gray coat. On very rare occasions this information is changed, or *mutates,* in an egg or sperm so that an offspring may have a light-gray coat. Since reproduction involves the combination of information from two parents, a wide variety of coat colors can arise from a few changes. In the shadows of the wood lot, however, a darker coat provides better camouflage, and mice with such a coat have a much better chance of survival. This means that more dark mice are around to pass on their dark-coat characteristic to succeeding generations.

If the surroundings should change so that the forest dies and the grass and brush take over, survival values change. Light coats become an advantage; the dark are eliminated and the deer-mouse population evolves into something else. In time this deer-mouse population breeds to a certain extent with other nearby mouse populations, producing a slightly different species. A deer-mouse population has become a cotton-mouse population, which has adapted to its new surroundings.

It is precisely by a series of events like those just described that man is believed to have evolved from simple cells over the past 4 billion years. The ability of an organism to adapt to changes in the environment is certainly considered to be a property that life on any other world must possess. Examination of other planets in our solar system and speculation on how the solar system came to be have led scientists to believe that some of the planets have undergone considerable changes over the past 4.5 billion years. The ability to adapt to these changes would be an absolute necessity for organisms if they were to survive.

## 4. Separation from the Surroundings

It would be hard for us to imagine any living organism that is not separated from its surroundings by some kind of shell or boundary. Any organism that didn't have such a boundary would be indistinguishable from its surroundings, which would force us to call both the organism and its surroundings alive; therefore, we conclude that the fourth property on our list would also hold for life elsewhere.

## 5. Control Systems

Just as engineers have devised self-regulating control systems which are used to operate huge assembly lines, organisms have developed their own regulatory mechanisms. Such regulation is essential if all biological processes are to function effectively. Control mechanisms must carry out their tasks not only within cells, but also among the cells that make up an organism and in the integration of an organism with its surroundings, which may be continually changing. Study of two of these control systems—the central nervous system and the body's system for making and using hormones—has been a part of biology for a long time. More recently the study of intracellular chemical control has become important.

## 6. Conservation of Energy and Mass Laws

All the objects in the heavens that have been studied by astronomers reveal a common characteristic; they all obey the laws of physics and chemistry as we know them on earth. This fact makes it easier for us to generalize about the characteristics of living organisms.

Two natural laws important to all living things are the *conservation of energy law* and *conservation of mass law*. The first of these laws states that energy can be neither created nor destroyed, but only changed in form. The second law states that mass, or material objects, cannot be destroyed, but can be simply changed in form. (It should be noted, however, that mass can be turned into energy in certain kinds of nuclear reactions. This effect is described by Einstein's famous equation $E = mc^2$; here $E$ stands for energy, $m$ for mass, and $c$ for the speed of light.) Both the conservation of energy law and conservation of mass law play important roles in determining how living things will function.

The act of living requires energy, whether the living object be an organism with few cells found in the intestine of a whale or an organism with many cells such as a newborn baby; all such living organisms extract energy from food they consume by means of the chemical process called metabolism. If one agrees that the law of conservation of energy holds throughout the universe, then it is hard to imagine an organism that does not absorb or consume food from its surroundings, extract energy from it, and use that energy to power its living activities. It should be made clear that the word "food" here can also mean the fundamental chemical building blocks which were likely present at the origin of life on earth. Thus certain molecules that we do not think of as food today, such as ammonia and methane, probably served as "food" during that time when the complex organic molecules that made up the first living organisms were being formed. One organism's methane molecule is another organism's banana split.

Food energy is used in a number of ways. For example, in larger animals some of the energy is used to power the respiration and blood-circulation systems; however, a significant part of the energy obtained from food eaten by an animal is used to break down the foodstuff itself into simpler molecules, which are then used to build new structures for the organism and replace older parts as they wear out. In the same way that gasoline kept in an automobile's fuel tank stores the energy required to power that auto on a long trip, energy not immediately used in a living organism is stored in fatlike molecules in the organism. An organism that had no provision for storing energy in some way would, of necessity, have to continually absorb or consume food in order to maintain its life processes.

If mass is also conserved on other worlds, then any waste products left after the energy has been extracted from the food will be released from the organism into the surroundings. If the organism does not eliminate its waste products in some way, then it must store them—a process that has its limits.

In summary, then, it appears that on worlds where the laws of physics and chemistry as known on earth are obeyed it is reasonable to believe that life there would have most, if not all, of the six general characteristics listed at the beginning of this chapter. This does not mean, however, that the shape, structure, or method of extracting energy from food will necessarily be exactly the same for organisms elsewhere. Worlds on which the laws of physics and chemistry as known to us are not followed are unknown, and perhaps unknowable, to people on earth.

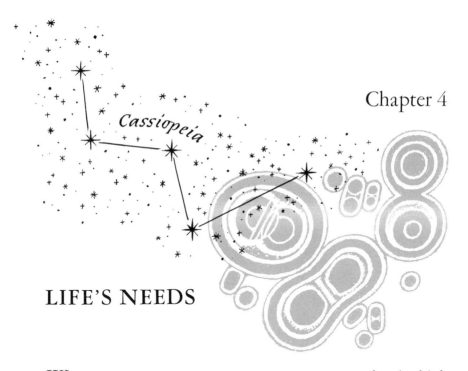

# Chapter 4

# LIFE'S NEEDS

WE KNOW that life could never exist on a star, for the high temperatures found on stars would kill any form of life. No living thing on earth has ever been observed to survive a temperature greater than $250°$ F. for more than a few minutes, and the coolest stars have surface temperatures of at least several thousand degrees.

However, any heavenly body that does carry life must be in orbit about a star, for all the energy in the universe originates in the nuclear reactions that create the light and heat emitted by the stars. Since, as was noted earlier, any organism must use energy in order to live, then the requirement that any body carrying life must be in orbit about an energy source—a star—becomes a necessity.

The heavenly bodies in orbit about stars include comets, asteroids, planets, and moons. Comets are collections of dust, small rocks, and ice particles; asteroids are minor planets. Both comets and asteroids may be excluded as bearers of life because of their small size. They have low surface gravity and therefore almost no atmosphere.

Every now and then a chunk of rock, a fragment of an asteroid or comet, successfully penetrates the earth's atmosphere and strikes the ground or ocean; such objects are called *meteorites.* These objects are of interest to people who are studying how life began on earth and its possibility elsewhere in the universe. In 1970 a group of United States scientists announced that they discovered in the fragments of a meteorite that fell in 1969 near Murchison, Victoria, Australia, seventeen amino acids, including six that are normally found in living cells. Amino acids are the building blocks used to make up the long-chain protein molecules. Prior to this discovery no one had really established with certainty that the amino acids found in meteorites came from space and were not simply earthly contaminants. The chemical-optical method used by this group established the space origins of such compounds in meteorites. This discovery strongly supports the theory not only that life on earth grew from a primordial ooze of chemicals present after the crust solidified, but also that if it happened here it could have occurred elsewhere in the universe. However, as exciting as this discovery is, it should be emphasized that amino acids are not alive, and that this report does not establish that meteorites could necessarily be a home for living things.

But there is one type of heavenly body we are certain about in regard to its ability to support life, and that is the planets. Generally included along with the study of the planets are their moons. Planets are bodies that give out no light of their own but are illuminated and heated by the star about which they orbit. Moons are generally considered to be natural satellites in orbit about a planet.

Because life is not known to exist anywhere else outside the earth, it is impossible to state the minimum requirements that life must satisfy in order to survive on other planets. It is impossible to know with certainty the needs of living things that might have evolved on other planets under conditions different from those found on earth. However, it is not impossible to state those conditions which would be required to support human life without being dependent on materials brought from another planet. Any planet which possesses these conditions will be called habitable.

A considerable body of information has been accumulated about the external conditions organisms living on earth need in order to survive. If, as many scientists believe, life elsewhere is based on cells built up of complex compounds of the carbon atom, then life elsewhere would probably have about the same needs as life on earth. That is, it is not clear that organisms made up of cells similar to the ones found in organisms on earth would be able to survive elsewhere in the universe if subjected to conditions that would be fatal to such cells on earth.

Temperature

There is a big difference between the temperature that humans can survive for brief periods of time and the temperature to which they prefer to be exposed. Most humans prefer to live in a region where the average annual temperature lies between

40° F. and 80° F. However, many humans ordinarily tolerate much greater temperature extremes, since they live in regions where the average daily temperature during the warmest season is greater than 100° F., while others live in regions where the lowest average daily temperature of the coldest season is below 15° F.

Certain blue-green algae have been observed to survive in water at 185° F., while another species has been found to tolerate water as hot as 149° F. and as cold as −2° F. Some ducks have been known to live for two weeks at −40° F. The arctic fir tree is capable of extracting energy from sunlight over a temperature range of −40° F. to 86° F.; however, most plants cease functioning below 32° F. but can survive temperatures as low as −80° F. An even more remarkable fact is that the seeds of some plants can withstand temperatures down to −310° F., though such seeds would not be considered to be carrying on the activities of a living organism.

## Light

Life on earth depends upon the natural harmony between plants and animals. Plants are only able to remove carbon dioxide from, and deliver oxygen to, the air if they are supplied with a particular kind of energy. They obtain that energy as light from our star—the sun.

The energy given off by a star is carried as waves of energy called *electromagnetic waves.* They vary in length. This may be observed by causing sunlight to pass through a prism, resulting in a spectrum of colors from red to blue. The waves

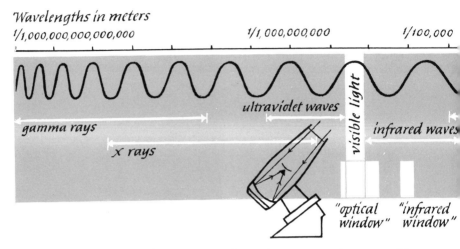

*Wavelengths in meters*

1/1,000,000,000,000,000          1/1,000,000,000          1/100,000

gamma rays

x rays

ultraviolet waves

visible light

infrared waves

"optical window"    "infrared window"

Many different kinds of energy travel as electromagnetic waves. The earth's atmosphere blocks most wavelengths of energy trying to get in or out; however, there are "windows" that pass certain wavelengths. Ordinary telescopes collect light rays entering through the "optical window."

producing the red band in the spectrum have longer wavelengths than those of the blue band. Energy is also carried by waves too long or too short to be seen by human eyes. Some of these longer wavelengths are called infrared waves, and they carry energy called radiation heat. The shorter wavelengths are called ultraviolet waves. Waves longer than infrared waves include radio waves; X rays have wavelengths shorter than ultraviolet waves.

Human beings can only see a very small part of the electromagnetic spectrum; that portion is called the visible portion of the spectrum, and it is contained between wavelengths as long as 760 billionths of a meter and as short as 380 billionths of a meter. It is from wavelengths lying in this portion of the spectrum that plants can obtain energy to carry out *photo-*

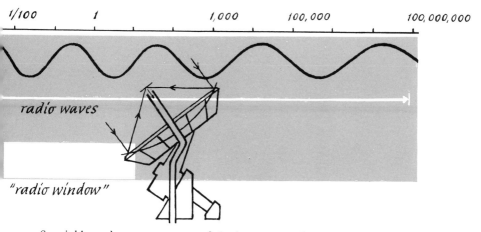

radio waves

"radio window"

Special heat detectors can record the longer wavelengths that come through the narrow "infrared window." Radio telescopes detect the even longer wavelengths of energy coming through the "radio window."

*synthesis*—that is, the use of light energy to absorb carbon dioxide from the air and water from the soil, and then to break them down into their fundamental atoms of carbon, hydrogen, and oxygen. The carbon and hydrogen are used to build additional plant structure, while the oxygen is returned to the air.

The intensity of illumination that plants must receive for active growth also falls between certain definite limits. If the intensity is too low, for example, photosynthesis cannot proceed fast enough to be useful; it has also been found (but not completely understood) that if the intensity is too high, growth can be reduced. For useful photosynthesis the illumination should probably not be greater than twice, nor less than about 1/200 of, the maximum illumination found on earth.

It is interesting to note that humans can see well enough to walk around if the illumination is only one ten-billionth the intensity of that which occurs due to direct and scattered sunlight on the earth. If the illumination rises to a level of about three or four times that of direct sunlight on earth, it generally produces pain in humans and hinders seeing; snow blindness is an example of the condition that results from too much illumination for human eyes.


## Gravity


According to Isaac Newton's law of universal gravitation, two bodies attract each other in proportion to the mass of each of the bodies, and the attraction is inversely proportional to the square of the distance between the bodies. The earth's mass causes it to pull down steadily on you and on every other object on earth; this pull prevents all the objects on earth from flying off into space. The further you move away from the earth, the smaller the pull it exerts on you. The earth causes all objects on or near its surface to fall toward it with an acceleration of one g (*g* for gravity). It is that acceleration that causes you to feel a pull. The pull is called *gravity,* and the strength of its pull on a body is measured by that body's weight. If you were on a planet with a mass greater than that of the earth, it would pull down on you with more force and you would weigh more. For example, if you weigh 100 pounds on earth, you would weigh 268 pounds on Jupiter. You would, of course, weigh less on a planet with less mass.

By putting a man in a chair on the end of a long arm and

swinging him around at high speed, it is possible to imitate the effect of being on a more massive planet. That is, the centrifugal force that he feels because he is spinning is in some ways like the additional force he would feel on a bigger planet. Human subjects have been known to tolerate, without losing consciousness, five times the earth's gravitational pull (5g) for periods of about two minutes. By reducing the force to only 3g the test period has been extended to an hour. At the end of a 3g test the subjects reported feeling great muscular fatigue. The life span of small animals was reported to decrease at gravitational forces greater than 2g. Both plants and insects can apparently tolerate extremely high g-levels—perhaps as high as 1,000g.

It would appear that most humans would not choose to live on a planet where the surface gravity is greater than 1.5 times the pull of gravity on earth. It would also appear, however, that organisms, over time, could adapt to whatever g-level existed on a planet so long as it was not too great. The structural strength of large mammals probably limits them to environments of less than 10g.

There does not seem to be a corresponding lower gravitational limit on the tolerance of human beings. That is, there is no conclusive evidence that a certain minimum level of gravity is required for the human body to function. There have been no negative medical results specifically attributed to the week-long periods of weightlessness experienced by Apollo and Gemini astronauts. However, there is still not enough evidence to judge what effect extended periods of weightlessness or reduced gravity—say several months or longer—would have on man.

## Atmospheric Composition and Pressure

The earth is surrounded by a blanket of air called the atmosphere. It is a little more than 78 percent nitrogen, a little less than 21 percent oxygen, and about $3/100$' percent carbon dioxide. This blanket of gases is extremely important to life on earth. It is the vehicle that carries carbon dioxide and oxygen back and forth between the earth's animals and plants. At sea level the atmosphere presses down with a pressure of 14.7 pounds on every square inch of the earth's surface. As one goes higher, the blanket of air becomes less thick, and thus it pushes down with less force. For example, at Denver, Colorado, at an elevation of 5,000 feet the normal atmospheric pressure is only 12.2 pounds per square inch.

Miners in the Chilean Andes live at an altitude of 17,500 feet and work at an altitude of 19,000 feet, where the atmospheric pressure is only about 7 pounds per square inch. Tests on human and animal subjects show that when the pressure drops to about 2 pounds per square inch, the body begins to swell, due to the formation of gas bubbles in the blood.

How great an atmospheric pressure the human body can tolerate has not been determined exactly. Experiments show that when the pressure reaches about eight times what it is at sea level, breathing becomes a very exhausting job. It should be noted, however, that aquanauts have been able to live for weeks below the ocean's surface breathing special mixtures of helium and oxygen at pressures exceeding twelve times the normal atmospheric pressure.

At normal atmospheric pressure humans appear to need an atmosphere containing at least 10 percent oxygen. The

Chilean miners at an altitude of 19,000 feet require an atmosphere that contains no less than 20 percent oxygen.

Just as it is possible to have an atmosphere with too little oxygen in it, it is also possible to have an atmosphere with too much oxygen. It has been found that if the oxygen content of the atmosphere at sea level exceeds 50 percent, oxygen poisoning becomes a problem. There are also limits on how much and how little carbon dioxide humans need to survive. If the carbon dioxide content of the air were to drop below 1/100 percent from the usual 3/100 percent, normal plant life would be in danger. If it were to rise above 1 percent, most animal life would be in danger. It is clear that man and the plants surrounding him are very sensitive to the atmosphere in which they have evolved.

## Water

Man and the earth's plant life are completely dependent on water. It is the one substance most closely tied to life of all kinds on earth. Furthermore, it is considered by many scientists to be one of the most remarkable substances in the universe. Any habitable planet must have fairly large open bodies of liquid water, for without oceans there could be no large rainfalls or snowfalls to provide supplies of fresh water. It is known that there is a certain minimum quantity of water that must be present on the surface of a planet before bodies of water can appear. If there were less than this minimum amount, all of the water would be in the form of water vapor like clouds, water absorbed on the surface, or water held between the solid particles of rock of which the crust is composed.

On the other hand, a planet completely covered with water, without permanent dry land, could hardly be considered habitable from man's point of view.

## Other Needs

In listing the requirements for a habitable planet, it is necessary to state what is required for human beings to survive on that planet. In order for a planet to be habitable, it is believed that other life forms must be present. All human food supplies, and probably the presence of free oxygen in the atmosphere, depend on the process of photosynthesis carried out by green plants. On earth green plants obtain from the atmosphere the carbon dioxide they need for growth and from water they obtain the oxygen they release back to the atmosphere. The atmosphere's supply of carbon dioxide is renewed mostly from two sources: (1) from the exhaled breath of man and other animals; and (2) from the millions of combustion processes taking place in man's machines all over the world. Any engine, furnace, or other device in which a fossil fuel such as coal, oil, or natural gas is burned releases carbon dioxide as a waste product. However, it has been noted that a planet could have green plants growing on it without having animals present if carbon dioxide were being released from the interior of that planet. The geologic evidence that has been found on earth indicates that its atmosphere was formed by gases, including carbon dioxide, that escaped from the earth's interior as it was being formed. Gases in small quantities still continue to escape into the earth's atmosphere—mostly water vapor and carbon dioxide—from volcanoes.

Other requirements for a habitable planet would probably include conditions not too different from those found on earth with regard to wind speeds, dust levels, radioactivity level, the rate at which meteorites fall, and the number and intensity of electrical storms.

Does our universe contain planets that meet all the conditions listed in this chapter for habitable life? No definite answer is available, of course, but the results presented in Chapter 1 indicate that there are more than 600,000 planets in our galaxy alone that could be considered habitable, even though man needs a very special set of conditions in order to survive.

# Chapter 5

# OTHER SUNS TO ENCOURAGE LIFE

THE UNIVERSE that is observed by man is mostly collections of stars gathered in big, and bigger yet, clusters or groups called galaxies. Our galaxy, the Milky Way, contains more than 100 billion stars, but astronomers have observed beyond the Milky Way countless other galaxies, some containing more and some containing fewer stars than ours.

It is from stars that all life forms derive the energy they need to carry out the process called living. Though not all stars have the qualities needed to allow life to survive on planets orbiting them, the number of stars is so great that millions of them in our galaxy alone do appear to have the right qualities.

## Stars

Stars come in a variety of sizes, energies, and ages. A star's two most important properties are its age and its brightness or surface temperature. It is not surprising to learn that yellow stars, which have a lifetime of about 13 billion years with a surface temperature of about 10,000° F., appear to have the best probability for life on planets in orbit about them. Our sun is a yellow star with a surface temperature of 10,000° F., and it is now about 5 billion years old.

A star is believed to form out of a cloud of dust and gas when gravitational attraction between the gas and dust particles causes the cloud to shrink. The collapse continues until the pressure raises the temperature within the cloud to the point at which the thermonuclear reactions that convert hydrogen to helium begin. The tremendous quantities of energy given off by these reactions set up a counterpressure in the center of the star that exactly balances the force of gravitational attraction. Most of the visible stars are in this balanced stage of evolution. When the lifetime of a star is given, it generally refers to the amount of time that it can expect to remain in this balanced state.

Stars may be grouped according to what can be learned about their physical and chemical properties with an instrument called a spectroscope. A spectroscope when attached to a telescope breaks up the light from the star being studied into a spectrum of colored lines, just as a prism breaks up sunlight. By studying a star's spectrum an astronomer can learn about its temperature, its motion, its chemical composition, and its age. By means of their spectra stars are grouped into spectral classes usually denoted by the letters O, B, A, F, G, K, M. (Astronomy students usually learn these letters by remembering the phrase *"Oh Be A Fine Girl, Kiss Me."*) The hottest and biggest stars are O-type stars, the next hottest are B-type, and so on, with M-type stars being the coolest and smallest. The sun is a G-type yellow star. It is neither extremely hot nor very cool.

A star's spectral class is further specified by the words *early* and *late*. These terms have nothing to do with a star's age but are used together with its spectral type to specify relative temperature differences. An early-F-type star is hotter than a late one, which in turn has a higher temperature than an early-G-type star such as our sun.

The length of time a star remains in balance can be calculated from the total mass of hydrogen in it and the rate at which the hydrogen is being consumed. The more luminous a star is, the faster it uses up fuel. Therefore, the most massive stars use up their substance most rapidly, and so remain in balance the least amount of time.

As a star burns its fuel in its central furnace, it begins to lose its balance, and gravitational attraction takes over. It first draws the gaseous body of the star in, heating up the interior and causing the thermonuclear reactions to spread to the outer layers of gas; these high-temperature reactions nearer to the outside of the star then cause the star to expand. In a relatively short period of time it starts to grow into a *red giant,* or a supergiant star. Once a star starts to expand, it grows so fast and gets so big that it would almost certainly burn up any planets in orbit about it.

After a star becomes a red giant, its evolution is not certain. Many red giants are known to pulsate—grow brighter and dimmer—for thousands of years. After a time all of the nuclear fuel within the star will be exhausted. The next step in a star's evolution appears to be the throwing off of its gaseous outer layers. This results in a tenuous *nebula*. In a time period on the order of tens of thousands of years the nebula will be spread very thinly in space, leaving only a relatively small and hot central core. What is left has become small because now there are no nuclear reactions to supply energy to stop the contraction of the star; the star becomes a *white dwarf*. The central temperatures of white dwarfs run into the millions of degrees, and the material that makes up such stars is denser than anything known on earth. The mass of one cubic centimeter of water on earth is one gram while the mass of a single cubic centimeter of white dwarf material is more than a million grams. Over the next 10 billion years or so the white dwarf continues to cool, all the while growing dimmer and dimmer. In time such stars lose all of their luminosity, at which time they are called *black dwarfs*. A black dwarf is completely cold and dead. It takes so long for a star to reach this state that it is doubtful if any of the stars in our galaxy have had time to become black dwarfs.

## Star Types Suitable for Life

The two most important characteristics of any star—its age and its surface temperature—are also the two most important factors in determining whether or not a star is a good candidate for having a life-bearing planet in orbit about it. It is somewhat easier to pick out those types of stars with the best possibilities by listing them in order from the youngest and hottest to the oldest and coolest:

| | |
|---|---|
| Type O<br>Type B<br>Type A<br>Type F (early) | Very hot stars that remain in balance for relatively short periods of time. |
| Type F (late)<br>Type G<br>Type K (early) | The stars in these three classifications are all good prospects for carrying life-bearing planets. |
| Type K (late)<br>Type M | Usually too cool, but can give off heat and light for very long periods of time. A few of them might be prospects for carrying life-bearing planets. |

Type O and early B stars burn so rapidly compared to the smaller, less luminous stars, that they remain in balance no more than about 10 million years. On the other hand, the much smaller and cooler M-type stars may give out energy steadily for as long as 100 billion years. None of the stars in the O, B, A, and early F groups has a stable lifetime of longer than 3.5 billion years; therefore none of them could provide suitable conditions to allow biological evolution to continue for a long enough period of time for intelligent organisms to appear on any of their planets—though 3 billion years is more than enough time to permit simpler organisms to develop.

If time were the only factor, late K and M-type stars would stand the greatest chance of having life-bearing planets. But these stars are not very luminous, and the habitable zones that such stars would create would be very narrow. A more luminous star can certainly warm up a bigger space than a less luminous one, just as a roaring fire can make a larger area in a cold room more comfortable than can a cigarette lighter.

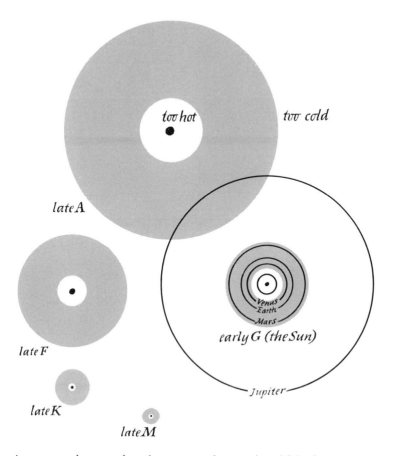

Regions around stars of various spectral types in which the temperature would be suitable for life. The late A-type star has the largest zone, but it does not remain in balance long enough for life to evolve. The habitable zone of our sun (an early G type) extends from the orbit of Venus to the orbit of Mars. If there are heat-producing reactions taking place on a planet, it might lie outside these regions and still be able to support life. Jupiter is suspected of having heat-producing reactions taking place on it.

The probability of finding a habitable planet in orbit about a late K or M-type star is reduced further when one considers rotational effects. More than 70 percent of the earth's surface is covered with water, and it is not unusual to assume that any planet which is going to be called habitable is also likely to have a substantial portion of its surface covered with water. Thus, if such a planet were close enough to a small star to receive sufficient heat and light to support life, it would also be under a very strong gravitational pull from that star. Recall that the closer two bodies are together, the stronger the pull of gravity between them. This strong gravitational pull acting on the planet's open water produces a tidal braking force that dissipates the planet's energy of rotation, so that it slows down and perhaps even ceases to rotate altogether. That tides do slow a planet's rate of rotation has been well established by studies done on the earth's tides. A planet that does not rotate and thus has no night and day, or has days that exceed ninety-six hours in length, is not likely to be considered habitable by man. Such a planet might attain surface temperatures that would cause the planet to lose by evaporation its large bodies of open water.

Taking into account both the stellar lifetime and the size of the habitable zone, it is possible to conclude that stars classified as late F, G, and early K are the ones most likely to have habitable planets in orbit about them. However, our knowledge of planets other than the earth is not sufficiently great at this time to completely eliminate the possibility of habitable planets being found in orbit about older and cooler stars.


## Nearby Stars of Interest

Galaxies are so much larger than anything that man usually thinks about, that astronomers have had to develop a special unit of measure to describe their size. It is called a light-year.

Light travels very fast. It takes little more than a second for it to go from the moon to the earth. The distance from the earth to the moon could be called a *light-second*. It takes about eight minutes for light to reach us from the sun, and thus one could say that the distance between the earth and the sun is eight *light-minutes*. But even the light-minute is too small a yardstick to use in describing distances in our galaxy or beyond. For these tremendous distances it is most convenient to use the *light-year*—the distance light travels in a year. One light-year equals 5,870,000,000,000 miles. That number can be read as 5,870 billion miles.

Our galaxy, the Milky Way, is a collection of stars that is shaped somewhat like a dinner plate. It is more than 100,000 light-years across, with our sun located about 30,000 light-years away from the center in one of the thinner sections of the dinner plate.

Because of the giant size of our galaxy, it is reasonable for man to begin his search for habitable planets with those stars that are relatively close to the earth. The distance to the center or the edge of the galaxy is so immense that most scientists believe it might be centuries, if ever, before man develops the technology that would enable him to personally visit those regions.

At present there is no way to photograph the planets of any star other than our sun. Even if such planets are in orbit around the star closest to our solar system, they cannot be seen on film for several reasons. The parent star's extreme brightness washes out any evidence of a planet, and the earth's constantly moving atmosphere introduces a fuzziness into all

A spiral galaxy in the constellation Leo. The arms, like those in a pinwheel, consist of dust and millions of stars. (Photograph courtesy of the Hale Observatories)

photographs of heavenly bodies. Someday a telescope may be located on a space platform or on the moon, where it would be free of the distorting effects of the earth's atmosphere. It is thought that such an instrument might film planets the size of those found in our solar system in orbits around nearby stars.

Even though it is not possible to see planets in other star systems from earth, there is another way to detect their presence. They give away their existence by something else that they do. They make their presence known by means of their gravitational attraction. Since any two masses attract, or pull on, each other according to their size and separation, the presence of a planet will disturb (very slightly) a star's path through the heavens.

As was discussed earlier, the only evidence now available to support the existence of planets beyond our solar system is that offered by Barnard's star, and many astronomers are skeptical of this evidence. The mass of the object that Van de Kamp detected in orbit about this star is only 50 percent greater than that of Jupiter. Because Barnard's star is of spectral class M5, which means that it is very old and very cool, it is thought that if there are any planets in orbit about it, they would probably not be habitable.

Stephen Dole, the Rand scientist who made the estimate in Chapter 1 of the number of habitable planets in our galaxy, has used the same type of reasoning to estimate how many of those planets are likely to be found within twenty-two light-years of earth. Of the initial 100 stars within this distance likely to possess habitable planets, some were discarded because they are too small, and some because they are so large that they are too short-lived. After carefully considering each star in the group and studying their characteristics, Dole made up a list of the fourteen most likely candidates. Five of the stars closest to earth that passed his test are:

| Star | Distance From Earth (Light-Years) | Spectral Class | Mass of Star Compared to Sun |
|------|-----------------------------------|----------------|------------------------------|
| Alpha Centauri A | 4.3 | early G | 1.08 |
| Alpha Centauri B | 4.3 | early K | 0.88 |
| Epsilon Eridani | 10.8 | early K | 0.80 |
| Tau Ceti | 12.2 | late G | 0.82 |
| 70 Ophiuchi A | 17.3 | early G | 0.90 |

It is interesting to note that the two closest stars to earth besides the sun, Alpha Centauri A and Alpha Centauri B, are considered to be very good candidates for possessing habitable planets. (Astronomers distinguish between the two stars in a binary star system by calling one *A* and the other *B*. Alpha Centauri is really a three-star system, but the third star is of the M5 spectral class and is therefore considered to be too old and cool to have a habitable planet.) Both the A and B stars are very similar to our sun and are very close to us by astronomical standards. But 4.3 light-years is still a distance that must be measured in thousands of billions of miles. Even if we knew there was a civilization in orbit about one of the Alpha Centauri stars, and a radio message was sent to it tomorrow, we could not receive an answer for almost nine years.

But is it necessary to travel out even 4.3 light-years to discover life? It may be possible that our own solar system harbors another planet that possesses at least some form of life.

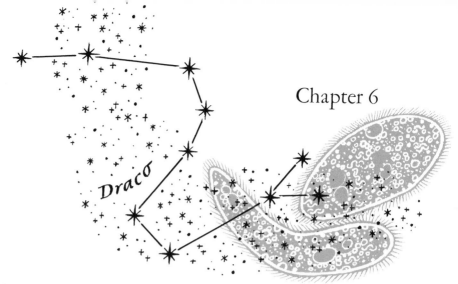

Draco

# OTHER CHILDREN OF THE SUN

ONE of the planets in orbit about our sun has life—even intelligent life—established on it. That planet is, of course, earth. And now life here has progressed scientifically to the point where it has begun to wonder seriously about the existence of life elsewhere in the universe. Since life has arisen on earth, why not on at least some of the other bodies in the solar system?

## The Moon

No one claims that there is life on the moon, but astronomers are constantly being surprised by discoveries from that apparently dead body. In 1958 N. A. Kozyrev, a Soviet astronomer, was making routine spectrograms of the crater Alphonsus on the moon's surface; much to his surprise he noticed a reddish cloud covering the main peak of the crater.

Thirty minutes later he noticed the cloud was gone. The spectrograms revealed that this cloud contained molecules of two carbon atoms joined together—a type of molecule not ordinarily found on earth.

The moon's small mass has given it a pull of gravity only one-sixth that of earth. Thus it has been unable to hold an atmosphere, losing whatever it might have had into space, until today no detectable amount exists. Any water on the moon has disappeared in the same way, so that now the moon's surface is bone-dry. The moon, being without atmosphere, lakes, or seas to store heat energy as the earth's atmosphere and oceans do, undergoes big changes in temperature from broiling hot to unbearable cold. At high noon of its two-week-long

Two branches of the Hygninus Rille, or valley, shown running into the crater Hygninus. The crater Hygninus is approximately 6½ miles in diameter and 2,600 feet deep. Objects lying at the bottom of rilles might be protected from the powerful, direct rays of the sun that reach the moon unfiltered by any atmosphere. ( Photograph courtesy of NASA )

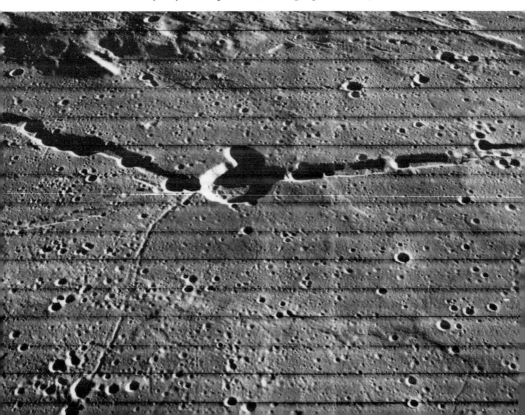

day, the surface of the moon may reach a temperature of 200°
F., but during the long night the temperature may drop to 250
degrees below zero. The lack of atmosphere also exposes any
object on the moon to a blast of ultraviolet rays and waves of
charged particles from storms on the sun, which would, in
time, destroy any living organisms exposed to these invisible
killers.

But there is more to the moon than its surface. Any object
that casts a shadow would be a barrier to the intense light and
radiation. However, because the lunar shadows move during
the month, as the moon rotates with respect to the sun, only
deep crevasses would be in prolonged darkness. But erosion
due to the solar wind and micrometeorite bombardment oblit-
erates such cracks in only a few million years.

The results of the Apollo flights have made available a
tremendous amount of information about the moon. Much of
the moon's surface appears to be covered with a thick layer of
fine dust. All of the moon rocks brought back by Apollo flights
are very old, having ages that range from 3.3 billion years to
more than 3.7 billion years. The oldest known rocks on earth
are about 3.5 billion years old, so that some of the moon rocks
evidently formed before the earth had completely crusted.
One of the rocks brought back by *Apollo 12* has been
especially intriguing to scientists. This piece of the moon,
known as Lunar Rock 12013 (for *Apollo 12,* rock 13), was
formed as it is now 4 billion years ago, but the components of
which it is made are probably 4.6 billion years old and could
well have been formed in the early hours of the moon's birth.
Absence of any water trapped in the dust or rocks suggests
that there has been no surface water on the moon at any time.

An *Apollo 11* astronaut's footprint in the soft dust on the lunar surface. (Photograph courtesy of NASA)

No evidence was found in the recovered samples of living, previously living, or fossilized material. But as man probes deeper into the surface of the moon and carries out more complex experiments there, who knows what he may find on earth's nearby constant companion?

## Mercury

The smallest planet and the one closest to the sun is Mercury. It is scarcely bigger than the moon (3,030 miles in diameter compared to 2,160 miles), and it is not very far from the earth, sometimes coming as close as 43 million miles. But it is extremely hard to observe, even though it is fairly elevations in these clouds temperature and pressure are about the same as those found on the earth's surface. In spite of the fact that there is little or no oxygen, the lower clouds of Venus appear to be as earthlike as any extraterrestrial environment that is presently known. Hopefully, future space probes will tell us more about this mysterious and well-hidden planet.

## Mars

Through the years no planet has held out more hope for harboring life than Mars. A little less than 100 years ago several well-known astronomers claimed that they saw long, straight structures on the surface of Mars. Some people called these canals, and a great debate began about whether or not there was life on Mars. In some ways the debate goes on today. The present conditions on Mars as we know them do not exclude life. However, it should be recognized that man himself would not find the planet very comfortable. The atmosphere is about 100 times thinner than the atmosphere found on earth, and it is mostly carbon dioxide. A man who stepped out unprotected from a space capsule into that atmosphere would be unconscious in a few seconds and dead shortly thereafter. Temperatures never get very much higher than about 70° F., even in the Martian summer, and they drop down to as low as −100° F. almost every night. There is no spot on Mars that stays above the freezing point of water (32° F.) during any 24-hour day. Mars—unlike the moon—has a trace of moisture on its surface. This planet, then, appears to be generally cold, almost dry, and without oxygen.

Perhaps the best-known feature of Mars is its polar caps. As

Photograph of Mars made by *Mariner* 7 at an altitude of 337,132 miles above the surface. The south polar cap, clearly visible in this photograph, is probably frozen carbon dioxide ("dry ice"). The photographs made by the *Mariner* spacecraft have never revealed the network of "canals" that some astronomers on earth began putting into their drawings a hundred years ago. (Photograph courtesy of NASA)

the Martian summer begins (it is twice as long as summer on earth) one of the polar caps starts to shrink, and a striking increase in the contrast between the bright and dark areas on the planet takes place. This change in contrast seems to move away from the cap toward the Martian equator at about twenty miles per day. The change in contrast chiefly affects those areas that were already rather dark, while the lighter areas remain almost unchanged.

For many years some scientists thought that the shrinking polar caps started a vigorous springtime growth of vegetation by making water available to plant life. Apparatus carried by the *Mariner* 6 and *Mariner* 7 spacecraft in 1969 was designed to detect the presence of methane and nitrogen. As Robert Jastrow, director of the NASA Institute for Space Studies, has pointed out, methane (natural gas) is released by decaying vegetation, but, being relatively unstable, it does not last very long in the atmosphere unless plants are present to continually renew the supply. Nitrogen, like methane, is a product of the cycle of growth and decay in living organisms. *Mariner*'s instruments failed to detect the presence of either gas. However, the instruments on board the spacecraft were incapable of detecting very small amounts of methane or nitrogen. If it had been on a spacecraft that flew by earth, the methane detection instrument, for example, could just barely have detected the methane in the earth's atmosphere. Thus a Mars flora could exist nearly as abundantly as the vegetation on the surface of the earth and still have escaped detection in this experiment. The *Mariner* experiments do not establish the presence of life on Mars; however, their negative results are interpreted to mean that life cannot be as abundant as, or more abundant than, life on earth. *Mariner* 7 did establish in the eyes of almost all scientists that the polar caps are simply frozen carbon dioxide ("dry ice") with only traces of ordinary ice present.

Sensitive instruments that have been trained on Mars have revealed that the dark regions are probably covered by small particles that grow in size and change color during the spring. These could well be small organisms. However, other explanations have also been advanced to explain the color changes. It has now been established that the dark regions are probably slopes. Carl Sagan has suggested that the slopes could be normally covered with a mixture of dust made up of particles of different sizes. Since fine dust generally appears brighter than the coarser grains of the same material, if a wind were to blow the smallest particles away, it would make the slopes look darker. Sagan suggests that perhaps such winds do blow in the Martian spring, while winds that blow at other times of the year have the reverse effect. The issue of the dust on Mars is far from clear. In the fall of 1971 vast dust storms were observed on Mars. As the dust settled, the dark regions became lighter, but they soon, in a way not understood, reverted to their previous darker color.

If any form of life is discovered on Mars, it will surely rank as one of the most exciting scientific discoveries that man has ever made. But such a discovery will not be easy. Cameras in orbit in artificial satellites about Mars would almost certainly not be able to detect very small organisms that lie below the surface. Even if the planet had larger plants or animals, it might be difficult to recognize them as living creatures from photographs made by satellite cameras, however sharp-eyed they might be. To detect life on Mars and to determine its nature would probably require the landing of an unmanned biological laboratory on the surface of the planet. Such a laboratory would be designed to sample Martian "soil" and to subject it to microscopic examination. Full exploration of the

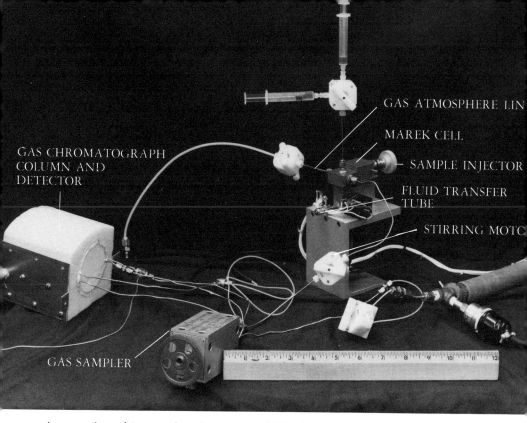

GAS ATMOSPHERE LIN

MAREK CELL

GAS CHROMATOGRAPH
COLUMN AND
DETECTOR

SAMPLE INJECTOR

FLUID TRANSFER
TUBE

STIRRING MOTC

GAS SAMPLER

An actual working model of a proposed life detector to be used on the *Viking* space probe which is to land on Mars. The apparatus is designed to take in a sample of the Martian soil and see if it contains any living organisms. The system gives its findings to the radio transmitter on the *Viking*, which then sends the results back to earth. (Photograph courtesy of NASA)

possibility of life on Mars may have to wait until human biologists will have landed on the planet and had an opportunity to carefully study what they find.

But what if Mars should prove to be a lifeless chunk of dead rock in a silent orbit about the distant sun? Most biologists claim that that would be a find almost as great as if living organisms were detected on the Martian surface. Wolf Vishniac, an experimenter on the biology instrument team of the

*Viking* project which is NASA's Mars lander program, puts it this way:

> It would for the first time place at our disposal a planetary surface which has not been turned topsy-turvy by living organisms. Which limiting factor prevented the development of such a complex chemistry as leads to life? Is it the lack of water? Is it the lack of nitrogen? Is it the excessive radiation. . . . Were I a biologist from another galaxy, sent to this solar system for the purpose of studying biology, I could wish for nothing better than to find two comparable planets, one with and one without life, one experimental planet and one control.

As his ability to explore the planets grows, man's curiosity will cause him to increase his observations of the red planet and eventually force him to pay it a visit. There is a good chance that without such a visit man will not be able to establish with complete certainty the answer to the question, "Is there life on Mars?"

## Jupiter

If you were approaching our solar system for the first time on a visit, what planet would you head for first? Not earth—that partially cloud-covered, tiny planet dancing around about 100 million miles out from the sun. You would, no doubt, go straight for Jupiter. Because our solar system really consists of the sun, Jupiter, and some leftover scraps. Even though Saturn appears spectacular, looking much like a baleful eye, it still has less than one-third the mass of Jupiter, and earth is 100 times smaller than Saturn.

Jupiter, the largest planet in our solar system, as photographed by the 200-inch telescope on Mt. Palomar, clearly shows the Great Red Spot. (Photograph courtesy of the Hale Observatories)

Jupiter is a lively place—it rotates in less than ten hours and sits in the middle of the nearly circular orbits of twelve moons —more than any other planet. It has a stormy atmosphere that reaches up thousands of miles from its surface. In fact, no one knows for sure where the atmosphere stops and the solid planet starts.

The atmosphere of Jupiter is composed mostly of hydrogen and helium, with smaller amounts of ammonia, methane, and probably water. The clouds are probably snowflakes of ammonia at very low temperatures. The most notable features of Jupiter are its light and dark bands and the Great Red Spot. The Great Red Spot changes in color from time to time, sometimes appearing pink or gray and sometimes brick red. It has been observed for more than 300 years. It is not known of what it is made or how it came to be.

No one knows what lies beneath Jupiter's atmosphere of hydrogen and helium, but astronomers do know that these light gases are fairly rare on earth. They are the commonest elements in the universe and are believed to be the material out of which all the planets were born. The earth has lost most of its hydrogen and helium because its relatively weak gravitational pull has not been able to hold these extremely light gases. But Jupiter, with its gigantic mass and a gravitational pull two and a half times that of the earth, has held on to its hydrogen and helium. The presence of these gases on Jupiter shows that the composition of the planet has changed relatively little since the solar system was formed about 5 billion years ago out of a giant nebula of dust and gas.

Could life begin and survive on a planet like Jupiter? Some planetary astronomers think so. They reason that the atmosphere of Jupiter must be much like the atmosphere that was on earth when life was forming here. With an atmosphere containing hydrogen, helium, methane, ammonia, and probably neon and water vapor, the only other thing required to form the complicated molecules of which living organisms are made is a source of energy. The fragments resulting from the breaking up of these simple molecules can then re-form into the long-chain molecules that are the forerunners of life. On earth this energy was probably supplied by either the ultra-violet rays of the sun or by lightning flashes. Because Jupiter is about five times as far from the sun as is the earth, sunlight there is only 1/27 as strong as on earth. But most astronomers believe that Jupiter's swirling and cloudy atmosphere produces huge electrical storms rich in lightning. These giant sparks could supply the energy needed to produce the complex organic molecules.

Life could not begin at the top of Jupiter's clouds because they are probably too cold. Some scientists believe that the bottom of the huge atmosphere might be too hot for life. The high temperatures there could be produced partly by the greenhouse effect and partly by contraction of the planet. As the planet contracts it would turn some of its gravitational potential energy into heat. But between these two extremes there might be a region where water could exist as a liquid. This is the potential *life zone*—a location that has all the conditions needed for life to begin and flourish. The chances that intelligent life will be found on Jupiter are not good, but on the other hand, so little information on what Jupiter is really like is now available that it would be foolish to rule out at this time the possibility of life being found there.

## Beyond Jupiter

The planets Saturn, Uranus, and Neptune are believed to be fairly similar in composition to Jupiter. At one time astronomers flatly ruled out the possibility of any life on these planets. They argued that the planets were extremely cold and had no oxygen at all, which would probably limit life there to extremely simple forms.

This argument is now open to question because scientists now know that the atmospheres of Saturn, Uranus, and Neptune can trap enough heat to give life a chance to begin. It is believed that temperatures on these planets could range as high as those found on earth.

Pluto, the planet furthest removed from the sun, probably has little or no atmosphere. Even if it has an atmosphere, it is still likely to be so cold as to make life there all but impossible, since the intensity of sunlight there is only 1/1,600 the intensity of sunlight on earth.

# Chapter 7

# LIFE AS WE DO NOT KNOW IT

IN AN EARLIER CHAPTER it was estimated how many stars might possibly have life-bearing planets. In our galaxy alone that number reaches into the hundreds of thousands. If there are that many potential homes for life in our galaxy, is it reasonable to assume that such life will be a copy of life forms found on earth? Most scientists think not.

They look around their own home—earth—and find thousands of different species of plants and animals. Even when they look at man, they find that he comes in a wide variety of sizes, shapes, and colors. Life moves down many avenues at the same time.

Man's ever-growing efforts in space exploration have uncovered a broad range of conditions existing on the planets in our solar system: the airless, waterless surface of the moon, which is alternately as hot as an oven and as cold as a freezer; Venus, with its thick cloud cover and a surface whose temperature approaches red heat; the dense, colorful clouds of Jupiter, held by a strong gravitational pull. Each of these heavenly objects is greatly different from the other, as well as being nothing like the earth. In other solar systems even greater differences than these can be expected to be found.

What can be said about the forms of life that might evolve on these other worlds? Some researchers believe that the early chemical processes which led to the origin of life here have been, or will be, reenacted on planets elsewhere, but this theory is far from proved. It is clear, though, that evolution by natural selection leads to a tremendous variety of life—all the way from the giant sequoia tree to the fine moss found on the sequoia's trunk, or from the huge whale slowly swimming across the equator to the tiny fleas dancing about the neighborhood dogs.

Two questions that many scientists have asked about life elsewhere, but have failed to find much agreement on, are: What are the chances that life could develop on a planet that has conditions similar to those found on earth? And would it be possible for life to develop on heavenly bodies that are extremely different from earth?

## Life on Planets Greatly Different from Earth

Considering the second question first, it must be stated that at this time no one knows if life could develop, or has developed, on a planet extremely different from earth. Further planetary exploration of our solar system may produce an answer to this question. Already, in 1972, a spaceprobe had been launched that was expected to fly by Jupiter in 1974.

In the next century or two man will certainly attempt to explore not only Jupiter but Saturn—the largest planets in our solar system. But this will be enormously difficult; indeed, the task will probably be one that will occupy human energies for a century or more. The great atmospheric pressures and violent storms of Jupiter will demand equipment more complex than anything developed so far. To develop such equipment it would be well, perhaps, to have a "Jupiter laboratory," with conditions similar to those of Jupiter but perhaps less severe, in which equipment could be developed and exploration routines perfected.

Fortunately, our solar system has provided us with such a laboratory—Venus, the nearest of the planets; this brilliant jewel in the evening sky has an environment in which man can indeed "warm up" for Jupiter. Venus's high surface temperatures and thick atmosphere will be extremely challenging, but Venus is not nearly as formidable as Jupiter, whose atmosphere may be 1,000 times heavier than the earth's. Many scientists believe that Venus will offer just the right amount of challenge to prepare man for his journey to that lumbering and colorful giant called Jupiter. For on Jupiter man will find—in addition to the very thick atmosphere of methane, ammonia, helium, and hydrogen—huge magnetic fields, violent storms, and a giant pull of gravity: in short a planet very different from earth.

And it will probably be when man first visits Jupiter that he will learn whether or not life can begin and survive on a planet unlike earth in almost every respect. It is almost impossible to predict accurately when such a visit could take place. Some scientists believe it could come before the first half of the twenty-first century has passed; others believe it will be a century or more after that. Whenever it does occur, it will certainly be one of the most exciting ventures that man has ever undertaken.

## Intelligent Life Elsewhere

Before discussing the possibility of intelligent life existing elsewhere, it is necessary to define what is meant by the term *intelligent life.* Most of the scientists who have considered this problem would probably agree that any form of life that could be called intelligent should at the least be able to visualize, imagine, and reason. Some scientists have suggested that the term intelligent life also implies the ability to communicate. Animals such as dogs and apes appear to have the ability to carry out tasks that require the ability to reason; a few apes have been taught to solve problems that necessarily involve making mental images.

Since a number of scientists agree that the universe probably has many planets with conditions very similar to those found on earth, does it automatically follow that intelligent life will sooner or later develop on such planets? This is another of those questions that have no certain answer. Some scientists believe that given enough time—say 5 billion years—manlike creatures will eventually evolve from the protozoans floating on top of the slime of almost any warm pond that contains the right atoms. Others believe it anything but inevitable. Carl Sagan put it well when he wrote:

> Are there other intelligences in the universe? Is the Galaxy filled with civilized worlds, diverse and unimaginable, each flourishing

with its own commerce and culture, befitting its separate circumstances? Or can it be that we are alone in the universe, that by some poignant and unfathomable joke, ours is the only civilization extant? [I. S. Shklovskii and Carl Sagan, *Intelligent Life in the Universe.* San Francisco: Holden-Day, Inc., 1966.]

Those men who believe that the existence of intelligence is not a unique and rare occurrence hold an idea that is in sharp contrast to what has been believed in ages past—that is, that man occupies a special place in the natural scheme of things. It was once thought that the Mediterranean Sea was the center of the world. Later on, once the earth's ball-like character was established, it was thought that the earth was the center about which the sun and the planets rotated. Then it was realized that the earth was a rather minor blob of stuff moving around a mighty central sun, and in due course we have learned that our sun is in no way privileged, but is rather a common type of star moving with a billion others around the center of our galaxy. Until quite recently it seemed that our galaxy was larger than other galaxies, but the more recent astronomical studies rate our galaxy about average in every respect.

So, many scientists have adopted as a guiding principle the idea that we are not specially privileged or unique, and for this reason alone they state that surely other intelligent beings exist in the universe. Adding to this argument is the currently accepted hypothesis of how our solar system came to be. This theory, called the nebular hypothesis, states that both the sun and the planets condensed out of a giant cloud of gas over the course of a few hundred million years. Whereas earlier theories suggested that the material to form the planets was pulled from the sun as a result of a collision or near-collision

About 5 billion years ago the material that made up the solar system existed in space as a very thin gas and dust cloud.

After several hundred million years some of the gas and dust coalesced into a ball, still surrounded by a thin gas disk.

With time the ball in the center and the disk became more compact.

Gravitational attraction between the particles in the central ball became stronger, compressing the parts together enough to start the fusion reaction that produces the heat and light given off by the sun. The material in the disk started to form into protoplanets.

The solar wind from the sun blew away the rest of the disk as the protoplanets formed into planets, leaving the solar system much as it is seen today.

between the sun and another star, the nebular hypothesis states that planets are a normal byproduct of star formation. While the nebular hypothesis is the present consensus viewpoint concerning the formation of the solar system, it must be emphasized that not all scientists believe it to be correct; there are some who believe that planets could form from interstellar matter gathered together by an already formed sun. However, most scientists believe that whatever mechanism formed the planets in our solar system, it was not a rare occurrence. Thus once again we meet the idea that there is nothing very special about us or our solar system.

Adding more weight to the probability of life elsewhere are the recent investigations of the origin of life on earth. It is now believed that the primitive atmosphere of a planet like the earth contained the atoms needed to create living organisms. In fact, the atmosphere found today on an outer planet of the solar system like Jupiter is believed to be very similar to the atmosphere that existed on earth when life began. (Indeed, on the outer planets it is extremely difficult to distinguish between a planet's atmosphere and its surface, since the planets are believed to be largely gaseous.) These atmospheres consist mostly of hydrogen and helium, along with smaller quantities of methane (one carbon atom and four hydrogen atoms), ammonia (one nitrogen atom and three hydrogen atoms); neon and water are also suspected of being in the atmosphere of the Jovian planets (Jupiter, Saturn, Uranus, and Neptune). This evidence strongly suggests that these planets were formed out of those atoms which make up 99 percent of the universe: hydrogen, helium, carbon, nitrogen, oxygen, and neon. Furthermore, four (hydrogen, carbon, nitrogen, and oxygen) of these same six atoms are those that occur most frequently in living organisms. It has been suggested that life on earth arose when the chemical composition of the earth's atmosphere was much closer to the average composition of the universe, and that some events which have taken place since then have changed the chemical composition of the earth's atmosphere.

Two conditions on the Jovian planets prevent the escape of very many gaseous atoms from their atmospheres, even if the atoms involved are the lightest of them all—hydrogen and helium. First, all of the outer planets are huge, which means they have very strong gravity forces to help hold their gaseous atmospheres. Secondly, they are very far from the sun, which means that their outer atmospheres are very cool and thus the atoms there do not have much energy with which to make an escape. The earth and the other inner planets are very different in both respects: they are smaller and therefore have weaker gravitational attraction for their atmospheres, and their atmospheres are much warmer because they are much closer to the sun and thus more energetic. Hydrogen and helium can escape from the earth today and probably could have escaped during the days when the earth was new. Even so, there must have been much more hydrogen available on earth at that time than there is now. Thus atoms of carbon, nitrogen, and oxygen were present on the primitive earth in molecular partnership with hydrogen—that is in molecules of methane, ammonia, and water.

J. B. S. Haldane in Britain and A. I. Oparin in the Soviet Union recognized during the 1920's that it would be extremely difficult to produce molecules out of which life could begin in an atmosphere rich in oxygen such as exists on earth today. But under hydrogen-rich conditions the formation of organic molecules would be much more likely. Furthermore, evidence of those early molecules would have long ago been destroyed. In the present atmosphere, which is rich in oxygen produced largely by green plants during photosynthesis, such molecules, over geological time, would be oxidized to carbon dioxide, nitrogen and water. If this theory is correct, the earth could have started with a Jovian-type atmosphere of methane, ammonia, and water out of which life began, and then over the eons of time this atmosphere could have evolved into to-day's atmosphere of carbon dioxide, nitrogen, and oxygen.

Those scientists who believed that life originated on an earth surrounded by an atmosphere rich in hydrogen-bearing molecules realized that they had a chance to test their theory with a simple experiment. It has been observed that the atoms in simple molecules like ammonia and methane will form more complex substances if first torn apart and then allowed to regroup. Ultraviolet light—that is, the light just beyond the blue wavelength that is found in sunshine; cosmic rays, which are streams of high-energy particles coming from space; and lightning are all believed to have been present on the primitive earth. Any of those sources of energy could have supplied what was required to tear apart the molecules found in the primitive atmosphere.

In 1953 Stanley L. Miller, an American scientist, placed in a flask of boiling water a mixture of methane, ammonia, and hydrogen gases. In another flask, connected by tubing to the boiling-water flask, he caused a 60,000-volt spark to pass through the gaseous mixture. The vapor was then cooled back to a liquid and boiled again.

Using very sensitive tests, Miller studied what was in the resulting mixture. Among other things he found several

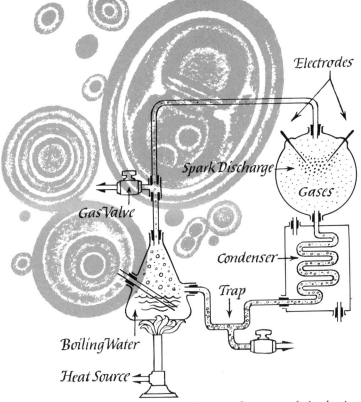

The apparatus in which Stanley L. Miller made some of the basic components of life from boiling water plus the gases methane, ammonia, and hydrogen. The mixture was then subjected to an electrical spark. After cooling the mixture Miller found amino acids in it.

amino acids and urea. Amino acids form the basis of the giant protein molecules that are in nearly all living things. Any protein molecule can be made from a combination of no more than twenty different amino acids. Urea is a very important compound formed in the bodies of most animals. Other experimenters soon duplicated Miller's work and found similar results, even when they replaced the electric spark with high-intensity light that imitates the ultraviolet rays of the sun.

It has been supposed that after amino acids were formed they then interacted with other groups of atoms perhaps leached out of nearby rocks by rainfall. Out of this warm broth of atoms and molecules came, in a way not completely understood, the nucleic acid called deoxyribonucleic acid (DNA). All life on earth appears to be based on the special properties of DNA and a closely related compound called ribonucleic acid (RNA). DNA, as described earlier, is a very long molecule found in the cell nucleus, and it contains in the ways its atoms are aligned the information, or blueprint, for the fabrication of every living organism.

Experiments have shown that once the first DNA molecule forms, the process repeats itself. This is reproduction at its most basic, molecular level. Thus it was but a step from the existence of the first DNA molecule on earth to the first simple living organisms, such as the protozoan. The slight changes from one generation to the next over several billion years that we call evolution eventually brought forth man.

But, it may be argued, just because man evolved from the atoms of a primitive atmosphere is no guarantee that man or other thinking beings will evolve on other earthlike planets. One answer to such arguments is the idea of mediocrity. This idea rests entirely on the supposition that there are hundreds of millions of planets like earth and that what took place here, far from being anything special, will surely have taken place on at least some of the earth's twins scattered throughout the universe.

## Intelligence Versus Humanoids

No responsible scientists believe that the large number of planets suitable for life that are believed to exist throughout the universe guarantees the evolution of human beings elsewhere. George G. Simpson, an evolutionary biologist, has presented an extremely strong argument against the occurrence of humanoids, or manlike beings, elsewhere. He states that once primitive life has appeared it is improbable that it will progress toward advanced, intelligent forms. Examining evolution on earth, he points out that the fossil record clearly shows that there is no central line leading steadily from a protozoan to a man. Instead there has been a continual and extremely complicated branching, which simply by chance resulted in man. He claims that the present species depends upon a very precise sequence of events taking place over a period of 2 billion years or more. If chance had caused evolution to proceed down a different road at any one of the branching points, man would not have evolved. Simpson argues that evolution is nonrepeatable, claiming that if man should wipe himself out, we cannot expect him to reappear millions or billions of years later. He logically concludes his arguments by noting: "This essential nonrepeatability of evolution on earth obviously has a decisive bearing on the chances that it has been repeated or closely paralleled on any other planet."

Simpson's arguments, of course, have not gone unanswered. Those scientists who doubt his conclusions claim it is not important whether humanoids are plentiful or nonexistent in the universe. They claim they are interested in the *occurrence of intelligent life.* Such life, they reason, does not have to appear in humanlike form and capability. That is, *intelligent life* could exist in a million different sizes, shapes, and forms, none of which may look like man.

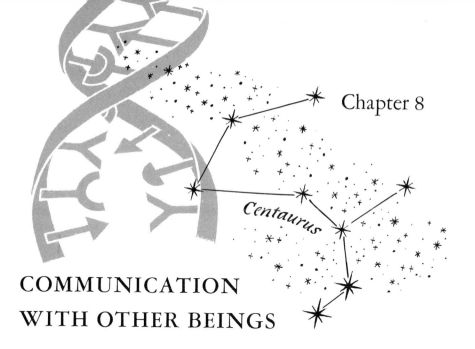

# Chapter 8

# COMMUNICATION
# WITH OTHER BEINGS

IN THE FALL of 1967 a group of workers at the University of Cambridge in England had recently begun to operate a new radio telescope. They detected some weak radio signals coming from a point among the stars, and on closer inspection discovered they were a series of pulses as regular as the ticking of a clock. Disbelief and excitement ran high as they started to systematically study the signals. Was this the contact from other beings on other worlds that so many people had speculated about? The scientists operating the equipment at Cambridge thought not. They believed it was some kind of electrical interference—perhaps from the ignition system of an auto, or a bad connection in a nearby refrigerator.

But continued study of the regular pulses eliminated earthly devices as their source. The scientists found that the signals were coming from a body no larger than a planet located relatively close to us among the nearer stars in our galaxy. It was becoming harder and harder to explain away these observations—perhaps they were artificial after all? But this explanation soon lost its attractiveness again, as similar pulses were located coming from three other directions in space. Furthermore, there was no planetary motion associated with these signals. After further study the radio astronomers concluded that these pulses were being generated in some way by the rapid rotation of a neutron star. [A neutron star (if it truly exists) is a huge collection of neutrons which would resemble a giant atomic nucleus. A single cubic inch of neutron-star material would have a mass of around a billion tons.] These pulsating sources of energy are now called *pulsars,* and they are under active investigation by scientists all over the world.

But if it had turned out that these signals were not coming from pulsars, how would scientists have gone about trying to determine whether or not the signals were sent by other beings? How would they have attempted to answer the signals? Are we now sending or trying to receive such messages? What are the prospects for us to visit other societies on other planets?

## Making Contact with Another Society

In the last century a European astronomer suggested that canals be dug in the Sahara desert in Africa forming variously shaped figures twenty miles on a side. At night kerosene was to be spread on the waters in the canals and set on fire. This was supposed to be the first step in establishing communications with observers on distant planets. Unfortunately, even if those observers had been on planets in our solar system and had possessed telescopes as good as our best, they would not have been able to see the flickering lights from the canals.

Today scientists consider three ways that might be used to make contact with beings on other planets: by radio, by intense visible light, and by making actual visits. Each of these means of communication, with the exception of actual visits, could be used to make contact with only a society that is about as technically advanced as ours, or more advanced than ours. It would be possible for man to visit less technically advanced societies, but probably more exciting to make contact with civilizations more advanced than ours.

## Radio

Great improvements in radio transmission and receiving equipment have caused most investigators to think this the most practical way of establishing contact with another civilization. The three main advantages of radio communications are: it is an extremely inexpensive way of transmitting information, the signal travels at the speed of light, and the signal can be concentrated easily into a rather small area of the sky. Man has no faster way of transmitting information than sending it at the speed of light—186,000 miles per second.

The rapid development in radio astronomy and the general growth in knowledge about radio signals have made it possible to narrow the number of channels—called frequencies or wavelengths—that might be used for communication in space. Suppose a friend of yours tells you there is a good program you should listen to on the radio today, but he forgets

The radio telescope of the Arecibo Ionospheric Observatory at Arecibo, Puerto Rico. The main dish of the telescope is 1,000 feet across; it focuses what it hears on a collector suspended by guy wires above the dish. (Photograph courtesy of Cornell University and the Bethlehem Steel Corporation)

to tell you what station is broadcasting it. Not knowing the station, you do not know what frequency to tune to, and thus you must listen to each station on the dial until you find it. Listening to space for broadcasts from another civilization is very similar, with the following important differences: the "dial," or number of frequencies that must be listened to, is much larger; the signal searched for would be much weaker; and there would be no familiar announcer's voice to help you know when you have found the program you wanted.

There does appear to be at least a partial answer to this problem, because there is a standard frequency that must be known to every technically advanced society in the universe. It is called the radio emission line of neutral hydrogen, and it was only discovered by man in 1951. Every now and then an electron in orbit about the hydrogen nucleus will change its orbit from one of high energy to one at a slightly lower energy. When this occurs it gives off the energy it no longer needs as radio waves with a wavelength of about 21 centimeters, or a little more than 8 inches. [Note that your home radio is sensitive to waves between 185 meters (600 feet) and 560 meters (1,830 feet) long.] The vast clouds of hydrogen floating through space set up a steady hum of radio noise at that "station" on the heavenly dial. Therefore it has been reasoned that the wavelengths near the hydrogen emission line should be searched. The search should not be directly on that wavelength—because the noise of the hydrogen would drown out any signal right there—but near it, or perhaps on double or half that wavelength. It seems reasonable to suppose that any technically advanced civilization would know about the signals that the electrons in orbit about hydrogen atoms give out; and so far as we can tell, the wavelength is the same throughout the universe. Because this effect has been observed at the farthest reaches of our galaxy and beyond, it is believed to be a truly universal phenomenon, and therefore it must be known to any civilization that has had more than a few decades of experience with radio.

But what kind of messages would we be likely to send or receive? The answer to this question has been thought about by a number of researchers.

It is important that the messages be clearly artificial and not natural in origin. A message might contain a series of prime numbers (a prime number is not evenly divisible by any number but itself or one). It might contain some simple sums, like:

This is a code that is easily broken with a little thought. The — stands for "plus," and the • — stands for "equals." A mathematical vocabulary could be built up in this way.

Philip Morrison, an American physicist who was one of the first scientists to suggest listening near the hydrogen emission line, has devised a method to send pictures using only dots and dashes. The problem with using such a system is that the receiver of the message would not know how to assemble it in a meaningful way. Morrison suggested that a "framing signal" be included in the message to assist the receiver in lining up the dots and dashes correctly. Below is an illustration of such a picture. There are a number of other schemes being considered for telling other beings what we are like.

Philip Morrison's suggestion of how pictures might be sent using only dots and dashes and a framing signal. The framing signal simply instructs a device like a teletype where to start and stop a line of dots and dashes. In that way the dashes are lined up to form an image; in this example a crude image of a man has been made with dashes.

## Light

A few years ago scientists developed devices called *lasers,* whose name is derived from the description of the device— *l*ight *a*mplification by *s*timulated *e*mission of *r*adiation. Such devices put out very strong light in an extremely tight beam that spreads very little with distance. This gives a tremendous advantage over an ordinary light beam, which has a tendency to spread and thus become dimmer with distance. In fact, a target to reflect a laser beam was left on the moon by the first Apollo crew, so that scientists on earth could accurately determine the exact distance between the earth and the moon by measuring the amount of time it takes for a flash of light from a laser to make the round trip.

Studies that have been done so far indicate that even if lasers were considerably improved, they would not be as useful as radio equipment in communicating with beings on planets in other solar systems. Two of the more serious problems associated with their use in this way are: ( 1 ) aiming them with sufficient accuracy at a distant planet; and ( 2 ) making them give out a signal that the observing civilization could distinguish from the light emitted by our sun. Neither of these problems is likely to be solved easily. However, there do not appear to be any major obstacles in using lasers for transmitting messages between planets in our own solar system.

## Unmanned Space Flights

Advances in the successful construction and launching of moon and planetary probes by man have been rapid. Each

The *Mariner* 7 spacecraft that made the photograph of Mars shown on page 68. Spacecrafts similar to *Mariner* might be sent to other solar systems to look for signs of life there. This *Mariner* weighs 910 pounds. TV cameras and electronic instruments are contained in the pod beneath the framework. The wings when deployed as shown give the Mariner a wing span of 19 feet. The upper surfaces of these wings contain solar cells which can convert sunlight into electricity used to operate the instruments and cameras on board the spacecraft. (Photograph courtesy of NASA)

year the unmanned vehicles become more complex and send back more useful information than those launched earlier. Many engineers and scientists who build these probes believe that in the not too distant future automatic probe vehicles will be launched from earth to go into orbit around some of the nearer stars, where they would become artificial planets.

Once in orbit about its new sun, a probe would automatically seek to make contact with any planets carrying intelligent life in its neighborhood. It could do this in the following way. Its radio receivers would search a wide range of frequencies looking for meaningful radio transmissions. Should such signals be detected, the probe would immediately record them and transmit them back toward the planet where they came from. This playback would undoubtedly attract the attention of the planet's inhabitants to the probe. The important thing is that this society would now know it had been contacted by a messenger from a distant civilization.

After the beings on the alien planet realized that another civilization was trying to contact them by means of the unmanned probe, a conversation, of sorts, could be established. The probe would be designed to transmit a lot of information about our galaxy, our solar system, and us. It would do this by broadcasting information that had been stored on magnetic tape, or some other system of information storage, on board the probe. The probe's transmitters could even be designed to send out television signals. Perhaps they would send pictures of the constellation in which the probe's star of origin (our sun) is located. The use of such unmanned probes would only work with a civilization technically advanced to the point where it could make some sense of the signals it received.

It would not be necessary for the probe to inform us of the success of its mission. Once the newly discovered society had received the probe's transmission about us, it could decide whether or not it wanted to get in touch with us. If the other society was as technically advanced as we are, it would have no difficulty in establishing direct communication with our civilization on earth.

If man wanted to be sure to keep track of his probes, it

would also be possible for him to set up a system of relay stations to funnel back to earth information from various star probes. It is not too difficult to imagine a giant network of intelligent civilizations held in contact by a series of relay stations posted about the galaxy.

## Manned Visits to Other Societies

There are a number of things that cannot be done by simply exchanging messages between societies on different worlds. Such exchanges do not permit the exploration of things like nonintelligent biologies, or the exchange of material objects. They also exclude the possibility of contact between societies like ours and societies that have not reached our stage of technical development. For these reasons, then, our space program will probably always include direct manned exploration of other planets. For manned space trips are the only method available to us that would permit direct physical contact with other living things or beings.

Each year man's ability to launch more complicated manned and unmanned space vehicles increases dramatically. There is no doubt that the next years will see more manned space adventures to the planets that are relatively near to earth. A round trip to Mars or Venus need not last longer than a year; unmanned space ships have already flown by these two planets and sent back considerable information. Before the end of the century manned trips will almost certainly have been made.

If man completes his examination of the other planets in

our solar system and finds no other forms of life, he will surely be disappointed. But he will also be faced with a tremendous challenge—he will, without doubt, resolve to look for life outside of the solar system. But when one starts to examine the possibility of traveling to planets in other solar systems, the problem becomes considerably more complicated. The distances to other solar systems are so great, that unless one travels at speeds approaching the speed of light one encounters travel times which may be longer than human lifetimes. Thus, if man is to easily visit other planetary systems, the rate at which he ages must be slowed down. Two ways to do this have been considered: by chemical means, or lowering body temperature, and by time dilation as occurs near the speed of light.

Research work on slowing down, or almost stopping, the rate at which things live has recently begun. It is now possible to preserve very tiny organisms for long periods of time by quick-freezing them at very low temperatures. Low-temperature storage of human blood is now done regularly. But the storing of a whole human being without killing him has never been accomplished. The reason for this has to do with the fact that almost all animals are composed largely of water, and water expands its volume upon freezing. If a living animal is chilled to a temperature where the water in its body freezes, the expansion does permanent damage to the cells that make up the organism. Ways to reduce this damage so that living humans can be placed in a state of suspended animation are now under study.

The second method of extending human travel is to take advantage of one of the consequences of Albert Einstein's special theory of relativity—*time dilation.* This remarkable effect would play a major role in any space flights where the speed of travel approached the speed of light (186,000 miles per second). The passage of time, as measured by the crew of a space vehicle, would be very slow when compared with the passage of time as measured by their friends and relatives on earth. As the crew traveled over distances of thousands of light-years, they would become only slightly older.

This effect, which sounds like something out of science fiction, has been confirmed many times by means of experiments. One of them is based on the fact that the earth is constantly being bombarded from space by the nuclei of atoms—a stream of charged particles called *cosmic rays.* One of the types of particles found in cosmic-ray showers is called the *mu meson.* The time it takes for a mu meson to decay or change its form at low speeds has been measured in the laboratory with certainty. If, for example, a mu meson were to enter the earth's atmosphere as a part of a cosmic-ray shower traveling with a velocity near the speed of light, but with a decay lifetime equal to its low-speed decay lifetime, it would never reach the surface of the earth; for that decay time is so short that the mu meson would have changed into another particle long before it got here. But mu mesons are detected at the surface of the earth all the time, because the time needed for them to decay when moving at velocities near the speed of light, as some of them in a cosmic-ray shower do, is much longer than the time needed for them to decay at slower velocities. That is, their very high speed has greatly lengthened their decay time because of the time-dilation effect.

There is no essential difference between biological time and physical time; both are subject to the same physical laws. Aboard a spaceship traveling at a speed near the speed of light not only would the passengers' clocks move more slowly than those of their counterparts on earth, but their hearts would beat more slowly and in every way they would age at a much slower rate—in brief, their awareness of the passage of time would be retarded. Traveling at these high speeds, in fact, acts as a metabolic inhibitor, but one that works on the whole spacecraft. Let us now consider how the phenomenon of time dilation would influence an actual journey to a star outside our solar system.

Imagine a spaceship that accelerates, or increases its speed, each second for exactly half the trip out to some distant solar system. During the second half of the trip it must slow down, or decelerate, if it doesn't want to just whiz by the foreign solar system. As was pointed out earlier, man does not tolerate high accelerations very well. So it would probably be wise to design the spaceship's engines to accelerate it during the first half of the trip and decelerate it during the second half of the trip at a rate exactly equal to the rate attained by any freely falling body on earth—that is, at about thirty-two feet per second per second. This increase in the speed of a falling body is caused by the earth's pull of gravity and is equal to one g. At this rate of acceleration the crew would feel right at home. Now, on the return trip, suppose the spaceship does just the same, accelerating at thirty-two feet per second per second during the first half of the trip and decelerating at the same rate during the second half of the trip as the ship approaches earth. Say this ship decides to visit Epsilon Eridani, which is 10.8 light-years from us. Due to the effect of time dilation, the crew on board the ship would age only about ten years, but the people left behind on earth would be twenty-four years older upon their return. If the crew decided to visit the Orion nebula, they would age only thirty years on their trip there and back, but 3,000 years would have passed on earth while they were away.

Acceleration and deceleration require energy, and energy comes from fuel. All of the investigations done so far reveal that there does not appear to be any realistic way to supply the tremendous amounts of energy required to continue the accelerations over the very long time periods required. The results of these investigations have caused most scientists to believe that for centuries to come manned space flights will be made only within our own solar system.

## Project Ozma

Before dawn on a clear, cold morning in the spring of 1960, Frank D. Drake, a young American radio astronomer, turned on the 85-foot radio telescope that stands in a meadow in Green Bank, West Virginia. The telescope's giant dish was pointed toward the star Tau Ceti, which we mentioned earlier as a possible sun having habitable planets in orbit about it. Mankind had begun the first major search that could lead to perhaps the most important discovery in its history—communication with another civilization.

Throughout the day the giant saucer of the radio telescope tracked Tau Ceti, its light invisible in the glare of the sun, across the West Virginia sky. Only the irregular hisses and buzzes that are constantly being generated in the vast reaches of space crackled through the loudspeakers in the control room. After Tau Ceti began setting in the west, Drake decided to listen to Epsilon Eridani. It, too, produced nothing but a low hissing and crackling sound in the speakers of the giant radio telescope.

After about 150 hours of listening the project was stopped because there had been no evidence of any signals from other star systems, and the telescope was needed for other work. Drake called this work "Project Ozma," after the name of the queen of the imaginary land of Oz—"a place very far away, difficult to reach, and populated by exotic beings." He and other radio astronomers hope to listen again to these and other stars.

## Is There Life on Earth?

If the planet earth were being observed by beings from another planet, what would they conclude about the possibility of life on earth? Carl Sagan, the planetary astronomer, has imagined the existence of a Martian astronomer. The Martian observer is supposed to have the most modern astronomical equipment currently available on earth. From his observatory he asks, Is there life on earth?

From Mars, the planet earth would appear as a very bright star, only slightly less brilliant than Venus appears from earth. Just as we see Venus going through phases like those of the moon, so could the Martian astronomer observe the phases of the earth as it swings around the sun. The earth would appear as a morning or evening "star" low in the Martian sky. One of the first things the Martian's instruments would tell him is that this planet is in an orbit somewhat smaller than that of his own planet and has an average ˙temperature considerably higher than that found on Mars.

But could the cities, dams, and other engineering works of man be seen from Mars? Because the earth's atmosphere is

A photograph of India and Ceylon made by the crew of *Gemini XI* during 1966 from an altitude of about 400 miles. Though these two countries contain more than 550 million people, no sign of life is evident at this altitude. (Photograph courtesy of NASA)

constantly in motion, even our largest telescope, the 200-inch reflector on Mt. Palomar in California, is able to photograph no detail smaller than about 180 miles across on Mars. However, the Martian atmosphere is much thinner than earth's, so it might be possible for the Martian astronomers to photograph things a few miles across on earth.

Photographs made of the earth from space reveal varying amounts of detail. But even photographs made from weather satellites from a distance as close as 400 miles show no evidence of living creatures. Though the shape of land areas is clearly visible, even giant cities are not apparent.

There is one characteristic of earth, however, that an astronomer on Mars might be able to detect which would lead him to believe there was indeed life on earth. Assume that the Martians are equipped with a modern radio telescope such as the one shown on page 92. If the Martian astronomer, like his earthly counterpart, chose to investigate the radio emissions of the planets in the solar system, he would be in for a whopping surprise. At wavelengths of around a meter (a little more than three feet) the insignificant planet earth emits almost the same amount of radio energy as does the sun in a period of low sunspot activity. In this wavelength range the earth radiates a million times more energy than Venus or Mercury. Further investigation would show that different regions on the surface of our planet give off radio energy unequally; for example, when Africa or South and Central Asia were facing Mars, the radio intensity would fall sharply, and when Europe and North America were facing Mars, the power emitted would increase sharply. If observations had been made over a long period of time, the Martian astronomer could make an even more amazing discovery: today the earth is emitting radio energy that is a million times more intense than what it emitted a few decades ago. At first the Martians would try to find a "natural" explanation for this phenomenon, but such attempts would eventually prove unsuccessful. The clever Mar-

Photograph of the area around Houston, Texas, made from an altitude of about 150 miles. The city of Houston appears in the left center of the photograph. Careful examination of this photograph reveals man's presence through, for example, freeways. (Photograph courtesy of NASA)

tians would come to realize that the radio emission could not be explained by the action of natural forces, but could only be produced by artificial means. They would conclude that intelligent life exists on earth.

It probably will not be necessary for space explorers to actually land on a planet in order to say for sure that living, thinking beings actually live there. Such explorers might actually be able to prove this with a relatively simple camera from as high up as 150 miles, if cloud cover is not too heavy. From this altitude bridges, dams, and roads are clearly visible. Therefore, it is now believed that even unmanned space probes will be able to orbit some planets and send back information on whether or not those planets harbor intelligent life. However, on planets that do not appear to have intelligent life a landing will probably be necessary to detect the presence of lower life forms. Not only scientists, but all the people on earth will wait for the results of these exciting experiments.

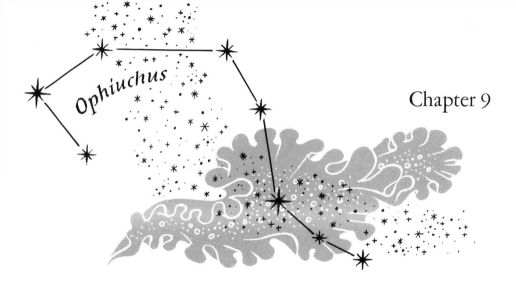

# MAN'S ROLE IN SPACE

IN 1961 JOHN F. KENNEDY, then president of the United States, pledged to put a man on the moon within ten years. In 1969 men indeed walked on the moon, placed there by the United States space program. Both before and after that historic event more and more citizens have been asking the same troublesome question—what is man doing in space? More specifically they want to know why the United States spent more than $40 billion in ten years to achieve a goal that many regard as little more than a super-circus stunt? They question the need for such expenditures when we live in a country beset with a number of serious social problems such as decaying cities, inadequate health care, and various forms of pollution which daily do irreparable harm to the environment.

A complete answer to these important questions is beyond the scope of this book, but many people, both scientists and nonscientists alike, have given much thought to them. Almost without exception they believe that in no other ten-year period in recorded history has man learned so much about his own planet, its natural satellite, the moon, and its sister planets, Mars and Venus, as in the ten years between 1961 and 1970. This information has added to man's storehouse of scientific knowledge, caused new industries to come into being based on space technology, and perhaps most important of all, given man a new perspective by which to view his activities on earth.

Some people have likened the first years of the space age to that period in the fifteenth century when man learned to cross the oceans and use them to explore portions of the planet which were unknown to him. But the pace at which space exploration has been taking place is thousands of times faster than fifteenth-century explorations, and the implications for man's intellectual and physical development are much more far-reaching.

Gaining first the ability to place a satellite in orbit about the earth and then to send probes off into space, man has been able to accomplish tasks he was simply not able to do before the beginning of the space age. Just a partial list of these accomplishments must include the following:

1. Almost continuous tracking of the earth's major weather systems, which has led to increased accuracy in weather forecasting.

2. Improved accuracy in almost every phase of map-making, which has enabled cartographers to fix precisely, for example, the exact locations of mountains in Antarctica, as well as ocean shoals and passages in the Bahamas.

3. The orbiting of numerous communications satellites, which has increased by many times the ability of man to trans-

mit radio messages, telephone calls, and television programs between distant parts of the earth.

4. The location of navigation satellites about the earth, which help pilots and ship captains to fix their positions accurately in all kinds of weather.

5. The collection of scientific data that were not available from instruments on earth but that are now collected routinely by instruments on scientific satellites; orbiting observatories have been built for collecting three types of information—geophysical (earth studies), solar (sun studies), and astronomical (space studies).

6. Interplanetary probes, which have sent back valuable information and photographs of the moon, Mars, and Venus; some of these data have changed opinions that have been held by astronomers for decades.

7. The Apollo missions to the moon, which have brought back priceless specimens of lunar soil that are now giving scientists new clues about how the solar system was formed.

8. But surely the most important thing that space has to offer us is a new frontier—a new region of the unknown. Some thoughtful persons, both scientists and nonscientists alike, argue that man must not lose his spirit of adventure. If indeed this is so, then perhaps exploration of space will be the ideal challenge. As man begins to look around the solar system, and in time even farther, it may turn his mind outward—away from thoughts of making war with his neighbors. Unlike war, which presents to society a well-defined goal—a goal that once won leaves society without a challenge—space is for all practical purposes without bounds. There will always be new worlds to explore and new challenges to be met.

## The Next Steps

Besides searching for signals from other civilizations, what might be the pattern of events that will follow as man looks toward the stars? It is certainly too early to describe it in detail, but it might go something like this. First there will be the explorers—the astronauts who possess a high sense of adventure and some knowledge of science. They will be followed by scientists eager to collect information about worlds all but unknown to them. Certain planets might appear to be so inviting and interesting that engineers and technicians would then begin to construct on them citylike places, using tools and materials at present unknown to man. Last will come colonists from earth—people who are willing to try to create a new culture, a new world, from scratch. Would people really be willing to leave earth, a place they know very well, for the dangers of an unknown planet? On the basis of history the answer must be yes. In the past century alone millions left the Europe they knew for an America they had heard but little about. There will always be those who are willing to try someplace new because they hope it will offer them more opportunities than their former homes or because they thrive on adventure.

What might these colonists do on other worlds? What fruits, vegetables, and grains might they grow near the Great Red Spot of Jupiter? What will the cities look like that our grandchildren's children might build beneath Saturn's rings? The real answers to these questions are almost impossible for us to imagine. Could the builders of early Alexandria or Miletus have imagined Tokyo, London, or San Francisco?

## What Has Man Lost?

Every year science has taken from man more and more of the things he thought made him special. Many believe that man's claim that he is the only reasoning and creative being in the universe must fall in the not too distant future. Where does this leave him? Is his civilization reduced to the significance of a collection of fruit flies swarming about a spoiled banana?

George Wald, a professor of biology at Harvard University, has given a very carefully thought-out answer to this question. He notes, as we have, that astronomers are convinced there are billions of other worlds and that biologists are persuaded many may be inhabited. But, Wald points out, it is man who has been able to imagine these other worlds. Without us, the universe might be, but not be known. We are not insignificant because we have proved ourselves capable of finding out some of the universe's secrets.

## What Can Man Gain?

Most scientists agree that it is not very likely that intelligent civilizations will be found close to us. This means that for the next century or more any contact that may be made with other beings will take place by radio. But because of the great distances involved, exchange of messages will take at least a human lifetime—or perhaps longer. Such time spans will not encourage the exchange of unimportant messages. However, there is perhaps a very great reward to be gained

An earth rise as seen by the *Apollo* astronauts as they came from behind the moon (shown in the foreground). The sunset terminator bisects Africa. (Photograph courtesy of NASA)

from establishing contact with another world, besides the one of learning that we are not alone in the universe. Our searching for, and successful finding of, other beings might turn up very durable civilizations that have conquered the problems of war, hunger, and disease. Perhaps we could learn from them how they did it. In that way an older society's wisdom could be passed on to a younger society, so that it might profit from the mistakes and successes of its more experienced elders. Surely, that would be the most precious reward that any civilization could find.

Thus the vastness of space might provide man with two priceless gifts—unlimited horizons to explore and the wisdom he needs to bring peace to this good earth.

# FURTHER READING

ANDERSON, POUL. *Is There Life on Other Worlds?* New York: Crowell-Collier Publishing Company, 1963.

CAMERON, A. G. W., ed. *Interstellar Communication.* New York: W. A. Benjamin, Inc., 1963.

CLARKE, ARTHUR C. *The Promise of Space.* New York: Harper & Row, Publishers, 1968.

DOLE, STEPHEN H. *Habitable Planets for Man,* 2nd ed. New York: Blaisdell Publishing Company, 1970.

JASTROW, ROBERT. *Red Giants and White Dwarfs,* rev. ed. New York: Harper & Row, Publishers, 1971.

KEOSIAN, JOHN. *The Origin of Life,* 2nd ed. New York: Reinhold Book Corporation, 1968.

SAGAN, CARL; LEONARD, JONATHAN N.; and the Editors of *Life. Planets.* New York: Time, Inc., 1966.

SHKLOVSKII, I. S., and SAGAN, CARL. *Intelligent Life in the Universe.* San Francisco: Holden-Day, Inc., 1966.

SULLIVAN, WALTER. *We Are Not Alone.* New York: McGraw-Hill Book Company, 1964.

# INDEX

# ABOUT THE AUTHOR

As Stanley W. Angrist began to study the available scientific knowledge on creation of the solar system for his first children's book, *How Our World Came to Be,* he came to realize that there were probably many worlds in the universe suitable for life. This idea of other homes for life fascinated him, and he began to seek out what conditions are now believed to be needed to sustain life and what is the best scientific estimate of the number of other worlds that could support it. The result of his efforts is OTHER WORLDS, OTHER BEINGS, his second book for young people.

Dr. Angrist is Professor of Mechanical Engineering at the Carnegie-Mellon University. He lives with his wife, Shirley, and his three sons, Joshua, Misha, and Ezra, in Pittsburgh, Pennsylvania.

# ABOUT THE ILLUSTRATOR

Enrico Arno has had a distinguished career as an illustrator of children's books. He was born in Mannheim, Germany, and educated in Berlin. In 1940 he emigrated to Italy, where he worked for book publishers in Milan and later in Rome. Mr. Arno came to the United States in 1947. He finds the subject matter of OTHER WORLDS, OTHER BEINGS fascinating to illustrate because "it intrigues both the scientist and the scientific illiterate," and also because it is a challenge to the imagination.

Mr. Arno lives with his wife in Sea Cliff, New York.